Food
Full of Life

Food
Full of Life

Nourishing Body, Soul and Spirit

GILL BACCHUS

Floris Books

First published in 2012 by Floris Books
© 2012 Gill Bacchus

Gill Bacchus has asserted her right under the
Copyright, Designs and Patent Act 1988
to be identified as the Author of this work

This book is also available
as an eBook

MIX
Paper from
responsible sources
FSC® C007785
FSC
www.fsc.org

British Library CIP Data available
ISBN 978-086315-915-2

Printed in Great Britain
by Bell & Bain Ltd., Glasgow

Contents

Acknowledgments

I would like to thank my husband, Peter Bacchus for his encouragement and help with his biodynamic farming knowledge in discussing and reviewing aspects of this book. Also Lis Alington, Gwenyth Wright and Christine Growse for their proof reading and comments. Thank you to Wendy Cook for her encouragement and her demonstration of exciting dishes made with organic food.

I thank Katy Waite for her line drawings and encouragement, and all the authors and publishers for permission to reproduce the illustrations.

Thank you to the pioneering organic and biodynamic farmers who have demonstrated how high quality organic food can be grown profitably, particularly to those mentioned in this book: Ray and Jenny Ridings, James and Annie Millton, Ian Henderson and his family, Dorothea Leber at Michael Hall School gardens, Ewen and Jan Willis of Fruit Forest farm, and the staff at Loch Arthur Camphill Community Farm and Laverstoke Park. To other members of the Biodynamic Farming and Gardening Association of New Zealand and Taruna College for teaching me about biodynamic farming and particularly to Peter Procter, Hans Mulder and Glen Atkinson, and to David Wright for his assistance.

I would like to acknowledge the assistance of Professor Mike Hedley and the late Dr Neil Macgregor of Massey University, New Zealand, with my research and literature search which I drew on for this book. I also drew inspiration and guidance from the research on inner quality of fruit and vegetables by Joke Bloksma and her colleagues at the Louis Bolk Institute, Netherlands.

Thank you to Sally Polson and Christopher Moore of Floris Books for their editorial assistance with the manuscript.

Dedicated to my grandchildren, Alistair, Andrew, Sarah and Jodie and to all the children yet to be born whose health will be affected by the quality of the food their parents and grandparents choose to eat.

Introduction

In this book I invite you to think about the quality of the food you eat. We often take a lot of trouble to select and prepare food to look attractive and desirable. Does it also leave you feeling satisfied for some time after eating it, and does it contribute to your health?

The effects on our health of the food we eat are now generally accepted. Food allergies, cancer, skin disorders, attention deficit and autism can often be helped by changing diet and improving nutrition. Emotional and mental states and intelligence have also been linked to diet. People are exploring specific diets and some eat according to metabolic and blood group type to improve their health. Consumption of dietary supplements and food fortification are increasing. But shouldn't we be getting most of our nutritional requirements from our food? In New Zealand and elsewhere, the Five-a-Day campaign encourages people to eat at least five servings of fruit and vegetables a day. The USDA Food Guide recommends up to thirteen servings per day for some people. We recognise that eating fruit and vegetables helps to alleviate problems such as obesity, diabetes and cardiovascular disease.

Food nutritional value is generally assessed by how much of the essential nutrients the food contains. Diets are generally chosen according to standard average nutrient content of each component. But nutrient content and taste in fruit and vegetables vary considerably, according to how and where they are grown. Modern farming methods, contamination of food crops with pesticides and nitrates, and genetic modification have all contributed to concerns about poor food quality. Farmers and growers are using increasing quantities of nitrogen fertilisers for larger crop yields. This can reduce the quantity of other nutrients in the crops and can also adversely affect other food attributes. Many 'minor' nutrients such as silicon, copper and boron have important effects on how plants grow and the nutritional quality of food products, and these elements are often lacking in our soils.

I became interested in how growing methods affect food nutritional value when working as a policy analysis for the New Zealand Ministry of Agriculture. I was asked to read and make a summary of public submissions on a proposed policy for organic farming. Many of those submissions claimed that food grown in this way is higher quality and better for our health than food grown by conventional means with fertilisers and chemical sprays. This led me to investigate what scientific evidence there is to back up such claims. Many scientists maintain that no nutritional superiority of 'naturally grown' or organic food has been established, yet a growing number of people say that they feel better and are healthier when eating organic food.

I was particularly interested to learn about the biodynamic farming system, which is based on concepts introduced by Rudolf Steiner, the Austrian scientist, philosopher and educator. Steiner also gave lectures on nutrition. These lectures, and books written by several doctors and scientists who further developed the concepts, provide a very different view of nutrition from those still commonly accepted. They advocate looking at energy processes that maintain life in plants and animals rather than measuring nutrient levels. After pondering these ideas for many years, and finding more and more evidence from other fields such as quantum physics, that provide similar concepts, I believe they are very pertinent to some of our nutritional and medical challenges.

The biodynamic farming system aims to balance the energies flowing up into plants from the soil and nutrients with energies flowing in from the sun, planets and stars. These energies were known to investigators in medieval times and now quantum scientists are seeing their effects. Biodynamic farmers spray a silica (silicon) preparation on to plants to help them absorb the light energies from sun and stars. I became interested in how this very dilute silica spray affects plants and their nutritional value, and tested its effects on lettuce nutrient contents for a Master of Science degree. I found some apparent effects, but because of large variations between plants and the small number of treatment replications, few of the results were statistically significant. I think a better designed investigation could provide more conclusive results. More recently scientists have been discovering important roles of silica in plant nutrition and human health. It appears to have a key role in improving protein quality and bringing more light energy into plants. We have a lot more to learn about how silica and light convey organisational energy to plants and soil.

My interest in alternative aspects of nutrition was stimulated, as for many people, when I had a brush with cancer. I realised that my eating habits had helped to make me sick. Exploring information about nutrition, I happened to listen to an old tape of a lecture by Ehrenfried Pfeiffer, a German nutrition scientist who worked for many years in the USA. He asserted that many of our health problems relate to a shortage of light in our food. This started me on a long journey of exploration to find out what he meant.

There are many phenomena that some people consider part of reality while sceptics dismiss them as unverifiable and not real. These include religious doctrines, astrology and homeopathy. After a conventional scientific education I have struggled for years to reconcile what I instinctively believe to be true with what science has shown to be true. I have gradually become more convinced that there is more to life than what we can see and measure by conventional science. Some people are healed through religious belief and others are healed through homeopathy. Homeopathically prepared sprays (containing no measurable matter) have a measurable effect on plant growth. Many dairy farmers use homeopathic remedies to heal their cattle. The cattle are unaware of the debate about whether they work or not!

Conventional science and technology have contributed immensely to mankind's nutrition, health and lifespan, making it possible to grow large crops and store them for year-round supply. But I do not think that we can solve all the health and nutrition questions that still abound without recognising that humans, animals and plants are affected by unseen energies that we need to understand. I have aimed to use information that has been verified by modern science as far as possible in this book. Some of the ideas I discuss have not fulfilled these rigorous tests because they originated with earlier scientists such as Paracelsus and Steiner who did not use current scientific methodology. It is very difficult to use conventional science methodology to measure and show relationships of life processes. I believe there is still a lot we do not understand about these life processes and we should not ignore observations and ideas that have not been verified. I think we need to ask questions and consider whether a more wholistic approach to nutrition would be helpful in tackling today's health and behavioural problems.

The book discusses how food quality is affected by the way it is grown, with examples of New Zealand and British farms, orchards and market gardens. It looks at various ways of measuring food quality and how buyers can assess quality. Relationships between silica, light quality, soil biology and plant protein quality are explored. We can learn to assess food by training our own senses of taste, smell and visual observation, rather than relying on laboratory analysis. We can learn how the different energies in plants can be seen in the way they grow and how they affect human metabolism when eaten. The book discusses how the formative energies in food affect our health and thinking. These energies can be enhanced or destroyed by different ways of farming, processing and cooking. They need to be in our food, to assist our feeling, thinking and consciousness.

Food and diet not only affect physical health, but also our mood and our thinking. Rudolf Steiner contended that if we want to develop our consciousness and increase our capacity to think, love and contribute to mankind's development, we need to eat food that is 'alive' and full of the energies needed to stimulate our minds and spirits.

I encourage you, as 'an eater of food', to consider some different approaches to nutrition. I present a number of questions and ideas, not as an 'expert' to give you specific diet recommendations, but to set you thinking. For example:

—what difference does it make if food is alive?
—what difference is there between vegetables grown in
    water and those grown in soil?
—is a vitamin a chemical or an energy?

Taste can be a good guide to food quality for someone familiar with how a good quality product should taste, but now that taste can be manufactured artificially it can be misleading. We can train our tastes and perception to be more discerning.

One of the best ways we can ensure we eat good quality fruit and vegetables is to grow them ourselves. It is time that we take responsibility for our own health and seek out good quality food that suits our needs. Otherwise we continue to be enticed by food processors to eat food that does not contribute to our health, thinking and behaviour. Our choice of food affects what we can achieve, how we think and the future health of our children, our grandchildren and our society.

PART 1.

GROWING HIGH QUALITY FOOD

1. Food Production Methods: their Effects on Food Quality and Our Health

Do you know where your food comes from and how it is grown? In traditional farming societies, people have an intimate connection with the food they grow and eat but for urban populations, food generally comes from a shop shelf. We can take a lot of trouble to choose a good diet and prepare interesting recipes, but good chefs know that however skilled a cook you are, you cannot prepare a good meal from poor food ingredients.

Nutrition and health

We live in a world where technology is so advanced that communications, complex industrial processes and household chores are achieved by the flick of a switch, yet the majority of people in the world suffer from malnutrition. The reasons vary: insufficient food, insufficient income to pay for food, poor dietary choices, but a further reason is less often acknowledged: poor food quality.

Much of the food consumed in more affluent societies is deficient in quality. It does not contain sufficient essential oils, complex sugars, vitamins and complex proteins with the right balance of essential amino acids to keep us healthy. Most of the ways in which food is assessed for quality do not show up these deficiencies, and we cannot always rely on our taste. We can be fooled into eating poor quality food through artificial flavouring additives.

There is increasing evidence that our food and diet contribute to ill-health. Obesity, diabetes, cancer, cardiovascular disease, eczema, asthma, food allergies – the list goes on and on. Nutrition has been found to affect mental and emotional states as well as physical health.

We are recommended to eat more fresh fruit and vegetables and wholefoods. As we have seen, the Five-a-Day campaign encourages people to eat at least five servings of fruit and vegetables a day. But some medical doctors and nutritionists advocate nutrient supplementation because the nutrients in fruit and vegetables currently available are insufficient to protect against infertility, learning disabilities and a range of illnesses. This is not a new concern. In the 1930s a dentist, Dr Weston Price, thought the tooth decay he found in people's teeth related to their diet. He compared the 'Western' diet with those of Eskimos and various African and Indonesian people who still ate traditional diets. People eating traditional diets were much healthier, with little tooth decay, and their food contained at least four times as much calcium, other minerals and water-soluble vitamins and ten times the amount of fat-soluble vitamins than Western diets of that time (Price 1939, pp.275, 276). Since that time, comparison of nutrient tables between 1936 and 1986 has shown significant reductions in the average levels of calcium, magnesium, copper and sodium in vegetables, and of magnesium, iron, copper and potassium in fruits (Meyer 1997).

There could be several reasons for this decline. Maybe plant breeders have inadvertently bred less nutritious strains through focusing on other attributes such as yields, fast growth and pest and disease resistance. A major problem is that plants are forced to grow too quickly without all the elements and energies needed for balanced growth. Genetic modification is promoted as the way to increase nutritional content of food, regardless of the dangers to our health and the environment. But some farmers have shown that food nutrient content can be greatly improved through working with nature rather than against it.

Most of us are well aware that we need to regularly consume plenty of vitamins and minerals and many people try a variety of diets. Even if we do manage to find the right diet for our individual type, and eat a well-balanced diet, with plenty of fresh home-grown or organic labelled fruit and vegetables, and reduce intake of harmful fats, sugar and processed food, it may not solve our health problems. Many people find they need to take vitamin supplements and other health foods to maintain energy levels and health. How many people do you meet who are really bursting with energy, and whose eyes are sparkling with health and vitality?

The situation is serious, it is time that we take charge of what we eat and learn to distinguish good quality food through using our senses of taste, smell and sight, and seek good quality food rather than fake food.

I have an eighteen month old grand-daughter who I visit as often as I can. It has been fascinating watching her introduction to eating food and what she enjoys and doesn't like. She enjoys most of her meals and particularly likes green vegetables and slices of orange picked fresh from the tree. My daughter has difficulty finding her foods suitable for breakfast, with most of the breakfast cereals containing a lot of refined sugar and artificial flavourings. We had a discussion about buying organic cow's milk. My daughter was not convinced that the benefits from it would be sufficient to warrant paying over twice as much for organic milk compared to the conventional milk. When I see my grand-daughter blissfully drinking her bottle of milk, I wonder about the farms the milk came from and what difference it might make to her growing body whether it was organic or not.

I think this is a dilemma many of us face: what are the benefits of organic food, and is it worth paying more for? We know there is a reduced risk of pesticide and other chemical contamination of organic food, and that it is grown with more care for the environment, but what about nutritional quality? Many scientific trials have compared nutrient quality of conventional and organically grown food. Overall their results have been inconsistent and inconclusive, although many of the tests have shown fewer nitrates, more vitamin C and some minerals in organic food (Heaton 2002). Some recent trials have found that organically grown fruits and vegetables have higher antioxidant activity (Ellis *et al.* 2006) and that organic milk contains more essential oils than non-organic milk (Mitchell *et al.* 2007).

Food production methods affect product quality and taste

Nutritionists recommend that everyone should consume several servings of fruit and vegetables each day. But no-one seems to mention the huge variations in nutrient content you can encounter in fruit and vegetables. The USDA nutrient database (USDA 2011) shows average calcium content of iceberg type lettuce leaves to be 18 mg, and iron content 0.4 mg, per 100g fresh weight. Corresponding figures for loose-leaf type are 40 mg and 0.9 mg. That is a big difference, and note that these are average figures and individual lettuces would vary a lot more than that!

Basic soil type and quality has a large effect on nutritional quality of vegetables grown in the soil. Another major reason for differences and decline in quality is the way food is grown, which is a focus of this book. Many trials have shown differences in nutrient content between lettuces of the same type, and of other vegetable types, grown in soil managed in different ways.

Let's think about the different ways of producing food. Are you aware that many of the leaf lettuces and tomatoes in the supermarkets are grown hydroponically in huge greenhouses? Lettuces grown quickly in nutrient solution in an artificially lighted glasshouse may contain more of some chemical nutrients than those grown in old-fashioned composted soil in the back garden, but they have insufficient exposure to sunlight to build the complex proteins and oils we need. I would like you to consider other questions which will be further discussed in this book. For example: do you think home-grown tomatoes generally taste better? Taste can be a good guide to nutritional quality.

Have you had the experience of broccoli quickly turning to a bad-smelling mush when cooked? This broccoli has been grown quickly with a lot of fertiliser, so has a high water content. It may also be bitter, containing high levels of nitrates from nitrogen fertilisers. When a plant takes up nitrogen it is transported from the roots to the leaves. The leaves use sunlight to convert the nitrates to protein. If large quantities of nitrates are absorbed by the roots, they are likely to be deposited in the leaves more quickly than the leaves can convert them. Some of the nitrates remain in the leaves and in the broccoli heads, making them bitter. The bitter taste and low protein content of such vegetables is not the only problem: nitrates can be converted to nitrites in our bodies. High levels of nitrites can interfere with the transport of oxygen with serious health effects.

Many of the fruits and vegetables we buy can contain high levels of nitrates. A dark, bluish green in leafy vegetables is an indication of high nitrate content. No wonder many children reject vegetables – they often taste bitter because of their nitrate content.

Large scale 'factory farming' methods of food production

Fruit and vegetables with high levels of water and nitrates are a consequence of modern farming methods that use soluble nitrogenous fertilisers to grow large plants quickly. Food production has become very large scale and industrialised to keep production costs low. Crops are grown quickly and cheaply by applying large quantities of soluble fertilisers such as urea and superphosphate. The plants have to take up these soluble fertilisers when they take up water. Soil conditions are created in which plants are unable to absorb other nutrients such as copper and iron. The plants are not supplied all the different trace elements and energies needed for a healthy plant and the food produced by them is deficient in these minerals.

Unhealthy plants easily succumb to pests and fungal disease. To prevent this happening the plants are sprayed with pesticides and fungicides, traces of which may remain in the harvested food products. Even the low levels of pesticides that food authorities consider 'safe' adversely affect many people. Hormone disruption and infertility have been linked to specific insecticides and herbicides (Walsh *et al.* 2000). Crops such as celery and apples are generally sprayed many times with pesticides and onions are sprayed frequently with herbicides.

This type of farming has the advantage of enabling fast, large-scale production for large urban populations at costs low enough for people to afford. These production methods do not always lead to the problems discussed above, and poor quality food. Some good farmers with high quality soil grow high quality produce on a large scale. But large-scale distribution organisation may mean that produce such as milk and grain is collected together from many farms for transport and processing. The good quality is mixed with poor quality and the end buyer has no knowledge or control over the quality of food they buy.

The animals that produce the milk and meat we eat may also have suffered from eating pasture and grain crops grown with too much fertiliser and chemicals. Cattle have a different digestion system to ours. It is a longer process, including fermentation in the rumen stomach. Soft, fast-grown grass and maize corn do not provide sufficient fibre to enable proper fermentation, so the cattle are not healthy and cannot produce good food.

Many farm animals are kept in buildings with little or no access to pasture, soil and sunshine. This is not only cruel and unnatural, but can lead to poor quality food. Chickens and pigs eat grass and scratch in the soil when they have access to it. They pick up a large quantity of beetles, worms and other soil organisms, which are a good source of protein for them. The soil they ingest contains natural antibiotics which keep them healthy. When kept on concrete floors they would succumb to disease if not fed artificial antibiotics.

A DVD titled Food.Inc. (Schlosser & Pollan 2008), that shows how most food in the USA is grown, has been circulating around the world. If you have seen it, you are likely to have been as disgusted as I was to see how much of the chicken meat and hamburgers consumed in the USA are produced. How can chickens crowded into barns, so fat they cannot walk and cattle fed an unnatural diet of maize corn, knee deep in manure, produce food fit for us to eat?

We need more information about what are the alternatives to this type of production and what difference they make. Many people experience food grown by biological and organic methods as providing more wellbeing, even though scientific studies have not shown much difference in nutrient content compared to mainstream food. Chapter 3 discusses how the nutrients in food are measured and whether they can show the full nutritional value of food. With so many people less healthy than they would like to be, isn't it time we took charge of our own health and find out how to recognise and source good quality food?

2. Some Farms and Gardens where Quality is Important

Where can we find good quality food? Most of us buy at a supermarket, where there is a large range of processed food, packaged in cardboard boxes, jars or plastic bags and containing a range of additives. Supermarkets have greatly improved their supply of fresh food in recent years. Most UK supermarkets now have their own quality standards, source a range of organic produce and provide information about the farms the produce comes from. In other countries such as New Zealand and Australia this information is not yet available and the main quality criteria seem to be unblemished appearance and freedom from bacterial contamination.

In European and Asian countries with long traditions of growing, cooking and eating food, there is still a basic appreciation of good quality food. At farmers' markets around Britain and many other countries, farmers and growers market their produce as high quality, with pride. Shoppers expect to pay for this good quality. Such vendors and their produce are less evident in 'newer' countries such as Australia, New Zealand and USA where price is the main concern, even for those who could afford to pay more. Buying local has the advantages that produce can be fresher than food that has to be transported long distances; fruit is more likely to have been ripe when picked; transport energy is minimised and buyers can find out where and how the food has been produced. But for many busy people living in cities, supermarket shopping is more convenient. Quality control and origin tracking systems are therefore important.

A growing number of people believe that pasteurised, homogenised milk from large herds of cows kept inside or in large yards has a lower nutritional value than fresh raw milk from pasture-fed cows (Mercola & Droege 2004). Organic dairy farmers generally find that they rarely have to call a vet to sick cows. Their cows are much healthier compared to cows that eat grass grown using soluble fertilisers. Do you prefer to drink milk that comes from healthy or sick cows? Fresh grass contains protein and oils that the cows can convert to beneficial fatty acids.

High quality products are usually produced by farmers who look after their soil, providing manures and composts that feed myriads of soil organisms. These soil organisms in turn feed the crop plants. This is important both for crop plants and for pasture that feeds farm animals. Farmers who look after their soil life are not all certified organic farmers, but many of them are.

The farming system that has come to be known as 'conventional' mainly uses fertilisers to bypass the whole cycle of feeding soil organisms with plant and animal wastes, so that they can feed the plants. This practice has led to the food quality problems discussed in the previous chapter.

Biological, organic and biodynamic farming systems

An increasing number of farmers find they can still make a good living by producing high quality products through biological, organic and biodynamic systems of management. Most people know that organic food has been grown without using chemical sprays such as pesticides and fungicides. Fewer know how it is grown. There used to be a perception that organic growing meant not applying any inputs at all. Generally the food grown in such a way is poor quality – looking small, diseased, and unappetising. Successful biological and organic farmers generally apply a range of organic manures and fertilisers and work hard at creating healthy, fertile soil.

Many people are confused about these terms – biological, organic and biodynamic. In the biological farm management system that originated in the United States, the farmer supplies mineral and organic fertilisers to his soil to feed soil organisms, which in turn produce the nutrients for plant growth in a form the plants can easily take up. A good biological farmer produces high energy 'nutrient dense' food through feeding these soil organisms. Many biological growers also feed plants directly with foliar organic and mineral nutrients.

Organic farmers fertilise the soil with organic fertilisers – compost and manures made from plant and animal wastes. They aim to use as little mineral fertiliser as possible and also find natural ways of managing weeds, pests and disease instead of using chemical herbicides, pesticides and veterinary drugs. A good organic farmer plans their whole system so that wastes are recycled and plants and animals are kept healthy to reduce disease problems.

Biodynamic farmers use the same methods as organic farmers and they also apply biodynamic preparations to boost soil and plant vitality. These preparations are made from specific plant and animal parts, according to suggestions made in a series of lectures by Rudolf Steiner (1993). Some are sprayed on the land and others inserted into compost and manure heaps to increase biological activity. A good biodynamic farmer builds a unique self-contained system which produces high quality food products. The farm becomes an integrated 'organism' with its own identity, just like each person has their own identity.

Organic and biodynamic farmers can be 'certified', which means they are inspected once a year to check they are complying with a set of standards. This certification provides a guarantee to the food buyer that the food has actually been grown to those organic standards. Look out for labels and stickers that display certification logos. Note that they don't guarantee the food is of high quality, just the way it has been grown. Food sold as organic that does not have this labelling may well be as good or better quality or it may be of low quality and not have been grown organically at all.

Some organic farms and gardens producing high quality food

Ray and Jenny Ridings have a commercial organic dairy farm, milking approximately 230 cows, near Ngatea in the Waikato area, New Zealand. Ray and Jenny took over the farm from Ray's father in 1989, following the normal progression at the time, of moving through the sharemilking process to land ownership. It was during these years that they began asking themselves questions about the methods they were using and how sustainable they were. As Jenny put it: 'We suddenly realised that to solve the problem of diarrhoea from the tail end we needed to change what the cows ate at the front end'. It was the realisation that the quality of the food (milk), they produced from their cows was influenced greatly by their farming methods that brought them to change to organic farming.

The farm is on flat, clay and peat land, drained by a network of ditches. The farm stands out from the surrounding farms of ryegrass paddocks, as the paddocks are lined with trees which provide shade, shelter and some fodder for the cattle. The paddocks also contain a diversity of grass species and herbs such as chicory, plantain and clover which provide a much better diet than just ryegrass.

In contrast to many conventional farmers who rely on synthetic fertilisers and boosters such as superphosphate and urea to grow grass, the Ridings aim to work with increasing the biological life of the soil, which in turn provides a nutritious sward of fodder for their animals. They prefer to 'provide feed that contains the necessary fibre and amino acids for good fermentation in the cow's rumen, leading to proper digestion, rather than the quick grown unnatural 'floppy' grass that passes through the cow at great speed, shooting out of the back end as coloured water'.

Ray and Jenny apply organic fertilisers such as a solution of seaweed nutrients which is rich in trace elements that are often lacking in New Zealand soils. Their cows thrive on the grass and herbs they eat and rarely get sick, in contrast to conventional farms where veterinary bills tend to be high.

Ray and Jenny firmly believe that it is their duty to provide a food for the consumer that is nutritious. They have applied biodynamic preparations to their farm to improve the quality of their pasture. They make long windrows of compost in which they put the biodynamic compost preparations, then spread the compost around the farm. In New Zealand dairy cows feed mainly on grass all year round, supplemented by some silage or hay in dry summer months and in cold winter months.

In 2008 the Ridings decided to experiment with using homeopathic sprays made from biodynamic preparations, including the horn-silica, on their paddocks during the winter, to improve grass quality. They were very pleased with the result, and so were the cows. Paddocks that would have lasted the cows two days lasted three days, and the cows showed their approval by not bellowing and asking for more grass when the Ridings drove past at midday (the 'drive-by test'!).

The quality of food that animals and humans eat affects the health and functioning of every cell of the body. Disease doesn't just appear by accident. To change their management to produce high quality milk that contributes to health was hard at first, it meant being different from neighbouring farmers. Ray and Jenny made it work and have encouraged and helped many other dairy farmers to successfully convert to organic management.

An increasing number of British farmers have not followed the trend of increasing intensification. Instead of keeping large numbers of animals indoors they have returned to the older ways of keeping animals in more natural conditions, with the aid of modern technologies. Pigs love to root and poultry to scratch, finding lots of little animals and herbage to eat. These little animals, such as beetles and worms, provide good protein, and the soil they also ingest provides natural antibiotics which help to keep the pigs and poultry healthy.

The poultry at Laverstoke Park Farm near Whitchurch in Great Britain spend most of their time outside, getting around 30% of their food from grass and insects. Cattle, buffalo and sheep graze extensive pastures and their pigs also live outdoors, with arks for housing. The animals and poultry at Laverstoke Park are of old fashioned breeds which take longer to grow than the modern breeds of animal kept by most farmers. This enables them to accumulate more nutrients and better taste. The numerous Great Taste awards and testimonials from top chefs they receive are a good indication of the standard they have achieved.

The aim at Laverstoke Park is 'to become self-sustaining and self-sufficient, producing the best-tasting, healthiest food, without compromise'. To achieve this they are creating the most ideal, natural, healthy environment that will enable their animals and crops to thrive. 'We follow nature strictly, but use the latest and best scientific research, techniques and equipment. To achieve a natural, healthy environment, biodiversity as well as slow-growing animals and plants are vital factors.'

Since soluble chemical farming has become the norm many farmers have forgotten about the value of plant and animal wastes for building fertile soil. Organic farmers turn those wastes into resources, building compost and manure heaps. When these have rotted they are added to the soil to feed soil organisms. Laverstoke Park has an eight acre compost site where they make all their own compost and compost teas. Compost teas are made by mixing a small quantity of high quality compost in water, to which various nutrients and a steady stream of air are added. The air and nutrients cause rapid multiplication of bacteria, fungi and other organisms from the compost. The tea is then sprayed on crops or pasture to boost the micro-organisms and nutrients that benefit plant health.

'By enhancing the healthy bacteria and fungi in our soils, this aids plants to absorb the nutrients effectively and that is what gets the nutrients from the soil to the plant.' They recognise that 'there are more living organisms in a handful of good soil than people on earth!' Soils are regularly analysed to ensure the right minerals and soil organisms are present. Laverstoke Park food products are regularly taste tested and sometimes also tested for Omega oils, amino acids and trace elements. This enables them to maintain a high standard of produce quality.

Many wine-grape growers around the world are turning to organic and biodynamic growing methods to produce top quality wine. Whereas conventional mass production of food has led to standardisation of products, winegrowers aim to celebrate their differences. A good wine has the *terroir* of its location – a unique flavour reflecting the particular soil, climate and other characteristics of that vineyard. *Terroir* can be enhanced through biodynamic management, which builds a unique property that best fits into the terrain, climate and ecology of that place.

James and Annie Millton were the first commercial fully organic certified winegrowers in New Zealand. Millton Biodynamic Wine Estate near Gisborne is now certified biodynamic with Demeter New Zealand. This certification is a guarantee to the consumer that a farm or orchard meets the Demeter standards. These include that the farm is treated as far as possible as a self-contained unit, recycling nutrients and building a fertile biological soil so that inputs do not have to be brought on to the farm. Biodynamic preparations are applied regularly. An inspector checks annually that the standards have been met.

James and Annie use biodynamic principles and preparations to grow their grapes. One feature they have worked on is to grow other flowering plants such as citrus plants among the vines to give fragrance to the vineyard, believing that this contributes to flavours in their wine. Their wine is full of interesting complex and delicate flavours and has won many international awards.

A further feature of biodynamic properties is that they should have as many different enterprises as possible, in contrast to the large monoculture factory farms of modern farming. This enables them to be more harmonious and self sufficient and more resilient to adverse conditions such as climate change. James and Annie have created a lot of biodiversity, with an area of pasture where they keep cattle. The manure from these cattle is used for making biodynamic preparations and to improve their compost.

Harmful fungus on vines can be a problem in grape growing. Instead of using fungicides or large quantities of copper sulphate to manage the fungus, James uses a small quantity of copper. He mainly relies on spraying a tea made from his compost on to the vine leaves. As the compost is made from crop residues, this tea contains beneficial fungi that naturally grow in the vineyard, which crowd out unwanted fungi.

James sees a harmony of earth, water, air and light in the Gisborne environment, which contributes to his vineyard. 'Sustainable wine growing is all about silica to give fragrance, clay to fill out the middle palate and give a sense of texture, and calcium to give length and a frame on which the year's qualities can grow in the bottle as the wine ages.'

James describes the concept of *terroir* as 'somewhereness'. I would like to see that term applied to all food products. I see that possibility happening, particularly in Britain, where farmers take pride in growing and marketing their own distinct brand of product, with unique taste and quality. They are working in the opposite direction to modern farming methods which aim to produce a very uniform product. It is easier and cost effective to use standard seed, a standard quantity of fertiliser and harvest a crop of uniform size that all matures at the same time, with as little variation from different soil types and environment as possible. But often these products are flavourless, nutrient-poor and uninspiring to eat.

I often feel very disappointed with the taste of fruit bought from supermarkets. A major reason is that to prevent fruit rotting before it has been transported, set on a shop shelf for a while, then bought, it has to be picked before it is ripe. Also, the fruit is generally grown in large, commercial orchards. Driving past such orchards, with rows and rows of carefully trained fruit trees and herbicide-sprayed bare ground I question whether good food can be produced from such a sterile looking environment. I buy fruit from a very different looking orchard, called Fruit Forest orchard. There, orange and persimmon trees are grown in between large avocado trees. The soil is disturbed and driven over as little as possible and plenty of good compost is made and distributed around the trees. The fruit is picked just as it ripens and is sweet and full of flavour.

I appreciate that this kind of growing would be more difficult and less time efficient than the conventional orchards – but have we sacrificed too much for cost and time efficiency? I think we have, if our main aim is to produce high quality, nourishing food to keep people healthy.

Grains are an important part of many people's diets. There has been an alarming number of people finding they are allergic to gluten in recent years. Why is this? Apparently, breeders have purposely selected for grains containing more gluten because it improves baking quality. The gluten is a complex molecule, difficult to digest, and it seems that people are unable to digest it properly, so it causes inflammation of the gut. I wonder whether modern farming methods have also contributed to this gluten indigestibility.

Milmore Downs farm near Christchurch, New Zealand supplies many customers around New Zealand with high quality dinkel (spelt) flour. Dinkel is an ancient grain related to wheat that has not been subjected to modification through modern seed breeding techniques. It contains just as much gluten as wheat flour, but the gluten protein has a slightly different composition, so some gluten intolerant people find they can tolerate dinkel flour. The farm also grows wheat, barley, oats and rye and keeps beef cattle and sheep. This diversity enables it to be self-sufficient as a Demeter certified farm. The farm takes part in a biodynamic grain breeding programme for barley and oats in conjunction with grain breeders in Europe to improve the nutritional value of the grain and its suitability for organic farming. The Henderson family who run the farm attribute at least part of the quality of their grain to the biodynamic method, in particular, regular use of biodynamic preparations.

The grains are processed into flour by a Zentrofan mill. The grain is ground against a basalt stone using a current of air which keeps it cooler than in most stone mills, so more nutrients are retained in the flour. The constitution of the grain is less changed compared to flour milled in large steel-roller mills, and the nutritious bran is included in the flour.

Stone grinding is slower than steel grinding, so modern milling is another example of nutrition being sacrificed for cost efficiency. Food prices have been driven down so low that better quality foods seem expensive. Those of us who can afford more should think seriously about whether we value our health sufficiently to pay more for better quality products.

Producing high quality food gives a great sense of purpose and achievement to all who are involved. Selling the produce at a farm shop enables the buyers to know where their food is coming from and to feel some involvement with the farm. Loch Arthur Camphill Community near Dumfries, Scotland, has a well-known farmshop that sells a large range of Demeter certified foods produced on the extensive farm. A happy, vibrant atmosphere at Loch Arthur results from the strong community life shared by residents and visiting volunteers and also from the farm being biodynamically run for many years, with biodynamic preparations applied frequently. This atmosphere is reflected in their high quality vegetables, cheese, bread, lamb and beef sold in the shop. They are one of the few producers of biodynamic pork in Great Britain.

Vegetables bursting with vitality are produced from dark, rich garden soil, in the old walled garden at Michael Hall School, Forest Row, Sussex. The garden has been nurtured and regularly fed with well-made compost for many years and produces a large range of vegetables. Their vitality reflects the enthusiastic personality of the head gardener, Dorothea, who puts so much energy and care into growing the vegetables. Every farm and garden takes on the characteristics of their manager, which is then reflected in the quality of the produce.

The schoolchildren who see this garden every day grow up with a picture of how good food can be produced, as well as health benefits from eating the vegetables. Part of the garden is used for teaching gardening to the school children. Demeter certified vegetables are sold at their garden shop. The aim is to combine beauty in the garden with growing an abundance of good biodynamic vegetables for the school canteen, the garden shop and the local community.

What do all these farms and gardens have in common? They are all loved, cared for, respected, caring for the soil, plants and animals. They have a biodiverse mix of plants and animals that the farmer develops into a harmonious whole system. The plants and animals are connected to and in harmony with the earth, their surroundings and the whole universe. These farmers care about providing good nutrition in food that tastes good for the people who eat their produce.

3. Scientific Assessment of Food Nutritional Quality

For large-scale distribution through supermarkets, appearance, uniformity and shelf-life are easier to measure and manage than actual nutrient content. I will discuss in Chapter 12 the question of how can you best assess nutritional quality of fresh produce before buying. In this chapter I discuss the various ways that research scientists measure food nutritional quality.

When scientists assess the nutritional quality of a new cultivar of a food plant or compare how different ways of growing a crop affects the nutritional quality, they perform standard chemical tests of nutrient content. Such tests often do not show much difference between nutrient content of food grown by different methods for a number of reasons. The weather, soil type, natural plant variability and other trial conditions can have a big effect on the results.

Standard nutrient tests

Mineral nutrients

Mineral contents are often used as a measure of food nutritional quality. Fruit and vegetables are important sources of minerals, particularly trace elements like copper and zinc. But fruit and vegetable mineral levels are very variable, depending on many factors such as the seed, soil and fertilisers used in growing and the weather. Organic growers sometimes claim that their produce contains more minerals. Some comparative studies have shown more particular minerals in organic compared to conventionally grown vegetables, while others do not – it all depends on the circumstances. I carried out a trial comparing lettuces grown with compost or with soluble fertilisers. When I analysed their mineral content, I found that although the organic lettuces scored higher for some tests, they contained less iron, copper and zinc than those grown with soluble fertiliser (Cole 2003, p.163). This would have been because I used a fertiliser that provided more calcium. The added calcium enabled the lettuces to take up more iron, copper and zinc. This really brought home to me that the results of any scientific research all depend on the particular circumstances of the trial. Next time you hear about the results of research showing that organic vegetables contain more nutrients or that they don't, remember that that result only applies to the particular circumstances of that trial. And if you want fruit and vegetables containing high levels of nutrients, you need to know that they are grown where those nutrients are provided.

Mineral content of our food is important. It is well established that we need certain levels of a large range of minerals for health, and that we should avoid harmful heavy metals such as mercury and cadmium. It is also important that the minerals we consume are in roughly the right balance. Many farmers know that if calcium, magnesium and potassium are not in the right ratios to each other in the pasture where their cattle eat, their cows get sick. There does not seem to be the same concern for nutrient balance in human food.

Vitamins and antioxidant activity

Scientists have linked health-giving properties of fruit and vegetables with their vitamin content. Some vitamins such as vitamin C and other plant compounds act as antioxidants and an alternative measure is the quantity of antioxidant activity found in fruit and vegetables. We have heard a lot about the damage that free radicals do in the body – highly reactive chemicals that can have devastating effects on protein cells if allowed to accumulate – and how certain antioxidant chemicals prevent or combat free radicals (Marieb 1998, p.79). So measuring the quantity of these chemicals or their activity in a plant product gives us an idea of how much it will contribute to our health. Vitamin C is an antioxidant, but when it is measured you only get a 'snapshot picture'. Compounds such as vitamin C are parts of constantly changing cycles in living plants, changing between different chemical substances. It is more helpful to measure antioxidant activity than the vitamin itself. In addition, there are other compounds in plants, such as flavonoids, that also contribute to antioxidant activity.

Growing method has been found to affect the contents of beneficial plant nutrients, such as antioxidants. One study found that the antioxidative activity of organic vegetables was 120% times higher than that shown by conventionally grown vegetables in the case of spinach, and 20–50% higher in the case of Welsh onion and Chinese cabbage (Ren *et al.* 2001). Concentration of several flavonoids (which act as antioxidants) in juices of the organically grown vegetables was 1.3–10.4 times higher than in conventional vegetables.

Protein

Crude protein level is often used as a quality measure of human and animal food, but this term includes various nitrogenous compounds as well as true protein. It is the true protein that is needed in the diet. Also, the relative quantities of each amino acid making up the proteins is important. Several amino acids are termed 'essential' because the body is unable to make them itself so they have to be in our food. If you eat protein that is deficient in one or more of the 'essential' amino acids, then your body cannot make much use of that protein. An 'amino acid score' has been developed to measure protein quality, based on the quantity of the amino acid that is most lacking (FAO/WHO 1985). However I have not seen many studies using this measure. In fact few studies measure amino acids or true protein content of food because these tests are time consuming and expensive.

Protein is needed for making all the different enzymes that drive chemical reactions in our bodies, and for building DNA and RNA, which transmit the body's messages and are important for reproduction. Plants that have been grown quickly using high levels of nitrogen fertiliser may have absorbed insufficient light to enable them to build good quality protein. Human fertility levels have dropped considerably in recent years (United Nations 2005) and many couples need to visit fertility clinics. Food supplies with low essential amino acid and true protein content, could have contributed to this problem.

Some crops are less able than previously to build good balanced protein and to transmit light energy (Shaw 1988). This decline can be attributed to genetic ability of modern crop plant cultivars, the way they are grown, and the effects of radioactive fallout around the world. Whether we eat plants directly or via eating meat and milk from animals that also depend on plants, we can end up with less light energy and less balanced protein than say, one hundred years ago.

Oils and fats

There has been a lot of contradictory information about what and how much fats and oils we should consume. Saturated fats, which are a high proportion of animal fats have been considered bad and unsaturated fats, mainly from plant and fish oils, good. But Sally Fallon of the Weston A. Price Foundation (Fallon & Enig 2000A) recommends a higher consumption of saturated fats. This is based on the research of Weston Price who found that people in traditional societies such as Eskimos, who consumed large quantities of saturated fats, were generally healthier than most people on a Western diet. As with most aspects of nutrition, the suitability of a particular diet for a particular person depends on many factors such as their constitution and lifestyle.

More recent research is showing that there can be large variations in oil content of crops, depending on methods of cultivation and the processing after harvest, and large variation in animal fats depending on what the animals were fed. Grain-fed beef is not the same as grass-fed beef.

There has been a lot of publicity about the benefits of Omega-3 fatty acids in reducing likelihood of cardiovascular disease, inflammatory conditions such as arthritis and mental conditions. The ratio of Omega-6:Omega-3 essential fatty acids in oils and fats is particularly crucial for health, rather than the quantity of Omega-3 consumed (Allport 2006, pp.115–50). Some deep-sea fish and some plant oils, such as flaxseed oil, have a high Omega-3 content and low Omega-6:3 ratio. Grass-fed cattle generally produce beef and milk with a lower Omega-6:3 ratio than grain-fed cattle, but there can be a large variation in this ratio amongst grass-fed cattle, depending on soil and pasture quality.

Taste

Taste is a useful method of assessment because people are more likely to buy and eat food if it tastes good. These tests can be made more scientifically acceptable by using a number of tasters in panels and training these panels to distinguish subtle aspects of taste. This reduces the subjective nature of these tests.

Often the large, unblemished fruit and vegetables in the shops have less taste than smaller, less 'perfect' ones. Or the taste may be different. I recently asked a group of school children to compare the taste of two sets of carrots – one bought in the supermarket, the other I grew organically in my garden. It appeared that the children who were used to eating home-grown vegetables preferred the flavour of the home-grown carrots: those were used to eating bought vegetables said that the bought carrots were sweeter, without the stronger 'earthy' taste of the others. Many of us have become accustomed to the taste of simple sugars in vegetables and the strong, artificial flavours in processed food. The more subtle, complex tastes of garden fruit and vegetables that our grandparents were used to are less well known. So although our own taste should be the best indicator of quality, we may not be able to trust it if we have grown up eating processed or poorly grown food.

Practicality and usefulness of nutrient analysis

It would be unreasonable to expect to be informed about the nutrient content of every piece of fruit or a vegetable: tests are time consuming and expensive. This is why supermarkets generally rely on their farm suppliers to keep production standards, rather than testing their produce.

Knowing the nutrient content of our food is of limited usefulness anyway. It would only be a rough guide as to whether it would fulfil your nutrient needs. The amount of a nutrient that is assimilated varies for each person and according to what other nutrients are eaten at the same time. For example, iron in the food can reduce absorption of other trace elements such as zinc and chromium and if you eat wholemeal bread, phytic acid in the flour reduces the assimilation of zinc. Researchers have found that such chemical interactions and poor assimilation by intestines that have become damaged make a large difference to nutrient intake.

A chemical test provides only a 'snapshot picture' of living products. Vegetables, pigs and eggs are living organisms. Instead of analysing the chemical constituents of our food, we can come to appreciate the plants and animals we eat. Isn't it better to assess the food we get from them as being a part of that whole organism?

Some alternative ways to assess food quality

Many people think there is a difference between an egg from a battery hen and one from a hen that roams free-range on pasture, or between soy beans that contain genes for Roundup pesticide resistance and traditional soy beans. Standard nutrient tests do not show any differences and any alternative tests that may show differences are considered unscientific.

Some of these alternative tests attempt to examine the whole food rather than chemical constituents. They are not accepted by most scientists because they have not shown consistent results when repeated many times. This difficulty is often encountered when researching living organisms. That is a characteristic of living things – they are never exactly the same. Chemicals are much easier to analyse consistently.

Brix level and nutrient density

Nutrient Density has become a popular, useful concept in the United States and New Zealand. Plants with high nutrient density have high dry matter content, containing high levels of nutrients. Generally, plants have to be grown well in a biologically active soil containing a good balance of minerals in order to achieve high nutrient density. Biological farmers measure a Brix index to establish nutrient density. Brix measures the soluble solid (mainly sugar) content of a plant product. It is used regularly by grape, kiwifruit and other fruit growers to test the ripeness of their fruit. Juice is squeezed onto the glass plate of a hand-held refractometer which measures the specific gravity of the juice, providing an instant reading. Some fruit and vegetable growers use this method to test for the nutrient density of their product, maintaining that it is a good measure of food quality. *The Brix Book* (Harrill 1994) provides more information and a table of optimum levels of brix reading for each fruit and vegetable. Brix level is a good guide, but, like other measures, generally only tells part of the story. It does not distinguish what nutrients are present nor how they are built into complex compounds such as proteins. It does not include oil content. Other measures like the acidity of fruit are also important: fruit with high sugar and low acid content tends to taste very bland.

Inner quality

Dutch researchers at the Louis Bolk Institute made a comprehensive study of apple quality (Bloksma *et al.* 2004). They investigated a large number of attributes of apples and compared many different quality measurements, both standard tests and alternative methods. They came up with an interesting concept of quality: food should have a coherent 'inner quality', which is achieved by a dynamic integration of growth and differentiation processes in a plant.

Think of the growth process as a plant pushing upwards and outwards in the spring and differentiation processes as when the plant forms flowers, fruits and seed and more complex oil and protein compounds. A food product from a plant in which growth has predominated tends to be soft and watery, whereas a plant in which there has been more differentiation gives a denser product with stronger taste. For some products one extreme is appropriate but generally it is better that growth and differentiation energies are balanced or 'integrated'.

In a further study of carrot quality (Northcote *et al.* 2004) the researchers defined a concept of Inner Quality, as being an extension of the common exterior quality criteria of appearance, presence of wanted and absence of unwanted substances, and hygienic standards. They said that Inner Quality refers to properties which result in a crop-specific product that is ripe, tasty and has sufficient storage quality. These properties develop during the growing season as a result of growth and differentiation processes and are dependent on the balanced and coherent relation between these processes.

Coherence is a term used by physicists to describe how well correlated two or more waves are: whether they show some kind of ordered pattern or harmony. I think most of us have a concept of harmony: two notes can sound harmonious or inharmonious when played together.

Look at an apple: can you appreciate the particular round form it has? What holds it all together in an apple shape? Can you visualise an 'apple harmony', some kind of energy that governs the growth and formation of apples? The way in which a plant is grown could affect how harmonious or ordered it is and how well energy flows through the living plant system. Biologists are finding that the amount of integration and organisation within cells affects how the cell responds to stimuli, the regulation of gene expression and cell development (Lloyd *et al* 1997).

Delayed luminescence

The coherence of healthy living cells is the basis of a method of measuring food quality developed by Fritz Albert Popp (1998). He used the principles of quantum optics in 'delayed luminescence' tests. He observed that every living cell emits very faint radiations of photons. When the cell is excited by a beam of white light, the photon emissions increase. Popp measured the pattern of how the photon emission reduces back to the normal rate after the beam is turned off. A healthy cell gives a characteristic graph pattern, different from that of a diseased cell. This method can distinguish healthy and cancerous human cells and food of varying quality. He found that potatoes treated with artificial fertilisers emitted biophotons in a less regular pattern than did organically grown potatoes. This method has also been used to measure tomato quality (Triglia *et al.* 1998).

This leads us to the question: does it matter whether our food is alive or dead? Such a question affects how we decide to measure food quality because a nutrient extracted and measured in a laboratory is a 'dead' chemical. The measurement does not show what is happening in a living cell, where nutrients are constantly flowing in and out and changing from one chemical substance to another. It does not show the coherence, the ordering, the energy flow in the food.

Effects of food on human health

Ultimately, the best test of food quality is how it affects peoples' health. The difficulties of ensuring that people eat only the particular food being researched have prevented much research being carried out on human subjects in the past. Now there is a focus on this research, led by the International Food Quality and Health Research Association. One study underway is the KOALA project: the Louis Bolk Institute and the University of Maastricht in the Netherlands are studying how the development of allergies in newborn children relates to lifestyle factors such as eating organic food (Louis Bolk

47

Institute 2011). Two-year old children consuming chiefly organic, as compared to those consuming conventional dairy products, were shown to have a 30% lower chance of developing eczema. Their mothers' breast milk contained higher levels of fatty acids that protect against eczema conditions (Thijs *et al*. 2010).

An interesting experiment was carried out with nuns in a German convent (Huber 2004). Over a period of ten weeks their diet was changed from mainly processed conventional food, to a diet of fresh foods and then to a fully Demeter biodynamic sourced diet and then back to conventional. A whole range of tests were undertaken including physiological tests to assess physical health and well being as well as a questionnaire based assessment of their inner state and spiritual well being.

Results showed clear benefits of moving to a predominantly biodynamic diet. General health levels were improved, fitness increased, calorie intake, blood pressure and stress levels all declined. The nuns reported that they felt better in themselves and were more able to think clearly.

This experiment was not carried out on a scale that enabled a full scientific analysis, but is an indication that different production systems could result in measurable differences in quality. Many other trials have shown some differences in nutrient content and in other attributes measured. As we come to understand living organisms better I think more differences will be found in food from different production systems. Meanwhile the observed effects on people who eat the food is probably the best measure of quality.

Have you noticed a connection between your diet and how you feel and think? I find myself noticing more and more clearly that the day after I eat too much sugary food or drink more than one glass of wine my mind is pretty foggy and I don't feel so good. The ultimate test of diet and food quality is how it affects your health, and how you feel and think.

4. Living Food – Earth, Air, Fire and Water

To appreciate how the production system can affect food quality we need to understand how the biological, organic and biodynamic systems might differ from the more industrialised systems of agriculture. What is different about biological systems that might result in producing food containing more harmonious energy? Does it matter how alive our food is, and what does this mean for our nutrition and health? I think these are the important questions that food producers, scientists and nutritionists should be asking and researching. A better understanding of how our food crops and domestic animals nourish us and keep us healthy will help us to grow or buy good quality food.

A growing number of doctors and scientists take a wholistic approach to nutrition. Rudolf Steiner taught that it is important that food be alive and be grown in enlivened soil (Steiner 1991, pp.113–14). He said that food plants should be nourished by living manure and compost, rather than by artificial mineral fertilisers. Food from such plants gives us the strength to build our own protein and fat and keep healthy. He said that children of parents who ate food from artificially fertilised plants will have pale faces rather than healthy complexions. This indicates a possible difference between hydroponic and soil growing systems: all the trillions of little bugs in the soil, fostered by manure and composts, are important for food growing, and in some way contribute to the nutritional value of food. Vegetables grown by hydroponics may contain all the right minerals, but they are less alive. Food that is alive contains a harmonious energy flow, it glows with little photons of light energy.

What is life?

First we need an understanding of what is life. Scientists have tried to define life in different ways over the centuries. The best way to understand life is to observe it happening in plants, animals and humans. When we look at a plant or a piece of fruit it looks solid and static. But if you compare an apple freshly picked from the tree with one picked several days ago, can you see a glow of vitality in the fresh apple?

If you look at a piece of fruit or leaf under a microscope you can see streaming movement – anything that is alive has movement. Plant sap and animal blood and plasma constantly flow, carrying nutrients and waste materials. Plants and animals break down food into chemical constituents, build them up to grow, then release them again as energy, in continual cycles. Whenever a living plant is analysed for chemical constituents, the constituents found are what happened to be there the moment the plant was destroyed – in the next moment they might have changed into different compounds. The chemical constituents and the compounds they are built into are less important than the continued dynamic activity of the whole cyclical processes.

Let's have a look at how plants grow. Modern farming and horticulture focus particularly on the minerals needed to grow plants, such as nitrogen, phosphorus and potassium. In fact, these minerals make up a relatively small proportion of the plant: most is built up from the carbon and oxygen they take into their leaves from the air, the water they take up through their roots and the light and warmth from the sun. Look around at the wild, uncultivated plants growing anywhere they can – they grow quite happily without fertilisers! They have the ability to grow in those particular environmental conditions.

Both Eastern and Western traditions have described the basic elements that support life. Aristotle classified these elements as earth, air, fire and water. These are very general terms, for example earth represents anything solid, water anything that flows. We can modify these slightly to think of the basic requirements for plant growth as soil, water, air, light and warmth. Later in this book I focus particularly on light, but all the other elements are needed as well. The important thing to remember is that all these elements are needed in the right balance for healthy growth – if there is too much water and not enough sunlight, plants rot: if there is a lot of warmth and light in the summer and not enough rain, plants struggle to grow.

As I write there is a feeling of spring in the air. There is a particular smell, a warm, earthy scent. Is this coming from the plants as they 'wake up' and start to grow? Plants emanate oils and gases they develop from the life processes within them. They draw up energies from the soil that connect and interact with energies from the sun, planets and stars and earth atmosphere. The air around plants often seems to be alive with unseen energies weaving around the leaves.

I feel a great sense of gratitude and reverence for the living plants and animals that produce my food. When food is seen as a collection of chemical substances, a source of calories or even as energy flows, it seems impersonal, a thing, to be treated in the same way as an inanimate object such as a table or your computer. Albert Schweitzer wrote about how an attitude of reverence of life affects our relationship with living animals and plants (Schweitzer 1961). This reverence, which he saw as a basis for morality, has largely been lost in our modern analytical and mechanical age. When you see a little plant struggling to grow in a gravel path do you reach for a chemical to kill it with or do you wonder at the tenacity with which it manages to live there?

Enlivened soil

Soil provides a lot more than minerals for plant nutrition. It provides the ideal environment for plants to grow in. A well-structured soil contains soil particles of varying size, with gaps between them called pores. These pores hold air and water which are needed by plant roots.

They are also teeming with microscopic life.

People often notice that walking about on a well-managed organic farm feels good. There is a happy, alive atmosphere from the diversity of plants and animals around and the lack of destructive chemicals. Also, it feels different underfoot. On a farm where a lot of machinery is driven around to spray various chemicals, the soil becomes consolidated and feels hard to walk on. An organic farm feels more soft and spongy to walk on because there is a lot of air trapped in soil pores with millions of soil organisms growing and feeding and working away there.

When giving his lectures to farmers, Rudolf Steiner spoke of 'enlivening the soil'. He described how if you use only mineral fertilisers you can only influence the soil's watery element, but not the 'earthy element' (Steiner 1993, pp.68, 69). In order to bring our food to the right energetic state so that we can develop 'inner liveliness', we need to fertilise the soil with compost, in which the nitrogen has been stabilised by adding lime and the biodynamic compost preparations. In Chapter 11, I discuss further this concept of inner liveliness. I think it helps to explain a difference between hydroponically grown vegetables and those grown in soil. Only when the plant is grown in enlivened soil can it really nourish us.

Soil micro-organisms – friends not foes

Bacteria, fungi, algae, all the myriads of micro-organisms that surround us in soil, air and water are vital for our survival. The common perception in our society is that micro-organisms are harmful to our health and must be destroyed with disinfectants, sterilisers, fungicides; we have an array of chemical weapons for this purpose.

In fact the majority of bugs in the soil are good bugs, working away at their tasks of processing waste and recycling nutrients. There are also many beneficial bugs on leaf surfaces, penetrating into plant roots, and in our intestines. Our gut bacteria play a vital role in releasing nutrients from our food so that they can be absorbed into our blood.

Soil organisms help to build a good soil structure so that as well as providing nutrients, the soil is porous, containing plenty of air and holding plenty of water, as the plant also needs air and water. When a plant or animal is healthy it is full of its own life which prevents bugs attacking it and bringing disease. Only plants and animals which have insufficient or unbalanced life energy of their own succumb to disease, so surely it makes sense to focus on keeping them healthy rather than killing all the bugs.

When pigs are kept in their natural environment in pasture and woodland, they rarely get sick. They root about in the soil, taking in antibiotic producing bacteria that protect them from disease. Pigs kept on concrete floors need to be fed antibiotics to keep them healthy.

When animals are kept on healthy pasture and when crops are grown in healthy soil, full of beneficial organisms, they generally stay healthy and produce high quality food. Growing our food with manufactured chemicals and keeping animals in unnatural conditions has caused a lot of problems and reduced food quality. I hope you will have a look at some of the organisms busily working in an active soil or compost heap to help you to see bugs in a new light, and respect the work they do.

The soil food-web

Some years ago an experienced microbiologist, Dr Elaine Ingham visited New Zealand from the United States to give talks to farmers and orchardists about soil organisms. The message she brought has transformed the way many farmers treat their farms in New Zealand. Instead of only considering how to make the pasture and fruit trees grow with fertilisers, they are now more aware of what is going on in their soil and they aim to feed and care for their soil organisms. They now understand that is the best way to grow strong healthy pasture and fruit trees. Generally, the more chemical fertiliser used, the fewer soil organisms are found in the soil.

Elaine Ingham introduced farmers to the soil food-web – a

system operating in all healthy soils, in which each species provides food for another set of species in a long chain of relationships. Some organisms break down plant and animal wastes, other organisms transform these wastes into nutrients that can be taken up by plants. The nutrients are circulated in a never-ending cycle (see Figure 4.1).

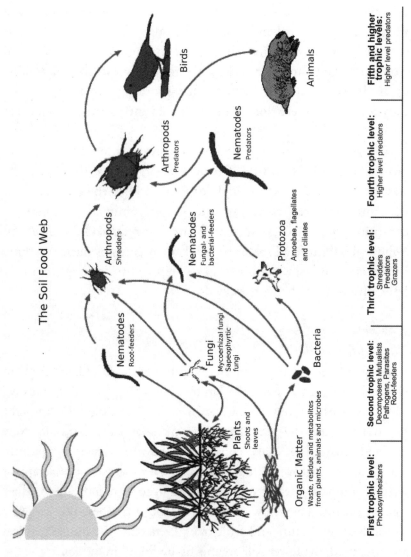

Figure 4.1: The soil food-web. From Soil Biology Primer, *Ingham et al. (2000), Soil and Water Conservation Society, USA, p.5.*

It's amazing to think that in a healthy pasture soil there can be 500 earthworms per square metre. A teaspoon of productive soil generally contains between 100 million and 1 billion bacteria (Ingham *et al.* 2000, p.18).

Several species of bacteria feed on atmospheric nitrogen, converting it to nitrogenous compounds in the soil. It has been estimated that bacteria convert many million tonnes of atmospheric nitrogen to for plant food. Most of the millions of tonnes of nitrogen fertiliser applied to farm soils around the world are not necessary.

We tend to see only the above ground parts of a plant and forget about the roots. But roots can be as extensive as the above ground parts of the plant. Their environment is important for the health of the whole plant.

Fungus organisms are also important for growing plants. A healthy soil contains miles and miles of fungal strands (hyphae) that help to feed plants. I am fascinated by mycorrhizal fungi (see Figure 4.2). These are fungi with long hyphae that surround trees.

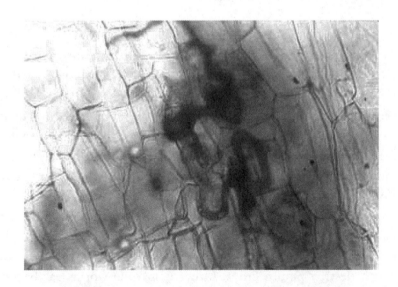

Figure 4.2: Mycorrhizal fungous hyphae and vesicles in lettuce root cells (blue stained, x 200 magnification).

These hyphae may travel long distances searching for nutrients, which they exchange with the tree roots for carbon that has been collected by the tree leaves. Sometimes these fungi send fruiting parts above ground, that you see as toadstools around trees.

Other species of mycorrhizal fungi grow their hyphae right into roots of many kinds of vegetable plants. When observed under a microscope you can see the hyphae penetrating into cells. In some cells they form storage vesicles which contain an oily-like substance. This substance is made up of phosphorus compounds which are essential nutrients for plants. Phosphorus carries energy that enables growth and metabolism. Research has shown that plant production is increased when these mycorrhizal fungi are active. This is particularly important for vegetables grown in New Zealand where most soils are deficient in phosphorus. Mycorrhizal fungi also produce a glutinous substance called glomalin which helps to give soil a good structure for growing plants. Every time the soil is dug or ploughed, these long fungal hyphae are broken and damaged, which is one of the reasons why no-dig gardening can be more successful than a lot of soil cultivation.

Thriving soil organisms improve plant and animal health
Cows and sheep that graze pasture grown by soil biology activity rather than by soluble fertilisers, are generally healthier and the vet bills are lower. This is important to think about. If cows eating pasture grown in this way are healthier, then it is likely that we will be healthier if we eat crops grown in the same way. It is also likely that the milk and meat from healthy animals will be of higher quality than that from less healthy animals.

In a healthy soil the beneficial organisms crowd out or inhibit harmful organisms. For example there are nematode worms that eat harmful nematode worms such as potato nematode worms which destroy potato crops. Other nematode worms eat bacteria or fungi, releasing nitrogen for plant food from them. An intimate connection between the plants, the micro-organisms and the soil is important for healthy plant growth. When vegetables are grown in water by hydroponics they miss out on this connection, although some bacteria do grow around the roots.

When a soil is alive with soil organisms it is a good indication that the elements of earth, water, air, warmth and light are all working together in a dynamic way to provide plenty of organising life energies in the soil. These life energies are needed to grow healthy plants that provide good quality food. Now we understand how plants and animals are made up of, and nourished by the basic elements of earth, air, fire and water, we can explore further the life processes that make them grow.

5. Plant Forms and Formative Energies

The first thing that strikes me when observing plants is the beauty, intricacy and diversity of their forms and colours. As I write I am looking at some feathery fern fronds and some bold bright daffodil flowers. Leaves are generally green, but what a variation in shades of green and diversity of shapes! Flowers seem to express the inner nature of a plant. Daffodil trumpets ray out bold bright yellow light that lifts and nourishes our spirits. The more I study the plants that grow to provide us with food, and also firewood, timber, paper, herbal medicines, beauty and even the oxygen we breathe, the more I am in awe of their gifts and feel a great gratitude to these plants. When observing plants I sense that there is something dynamic there that I cannot see.

When we enjoy a juicy apple or a fresh green salad we don't generally think 'this is giving me so much vitamin C or so much iron and magnesium'. We enjoy the taste and the sensations of crispiness as we eat. In a way we enter into a relationship with that food. Most chefs take a lot of trouble to source high quality supplies to cook with. They consciously assess the appearance and fragrance of fruit, vegetables, fish and meat. I suspect some of their assessment is an instinctive appreciation of the life in the food. The form, colour and fragrance of plants express the unseen life. In this chapter we focus on plant forms as an expression of life energies in them.

Environmental influences on plant forms

In natural environments, plant forms often reflect the dominant elements of that environment. For example the plants that grow in places where water is scarce tend to have small, shiny leaves that conserve water. In contrast, plants in wetter places have large lush leaves. Where the climate is hot and dry, only tough, small, narrow leaved plants like needle grass, and plants with tough outer surfaces like acacia trees and cactus, can survive. I find it hard to think of a plant that grows naturally in northern European countries such as Britain that is spiky and hard like the New Zealand flax. The spiky form reflects the brighter, harsher light in New Zealand. Softer, more rounded leaves are more characteristic in the softer light in Britain. Plant forms are also soft and rounded in the Tropics but much bigger, bolder and lusher in a hot, damp climate. The Aristotelian elements of earth, air, fire and water mentioned in the previous chapter provide the basic environmental influences which we can see in the plants around us.

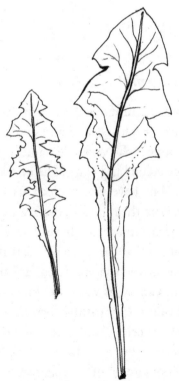

Figure 5.1: Dandelion leaves: on left from plant growing in light, dry conditions, on right from plant growing in a shady, damp place.

The same plant species can look different in different environments. For example the dandelion grows thin, indented leaves in a light, dry place, or more rounded leaves in a shady, moist place (see Figure 5.1).

Fruit and vegetable growers aim to provide good growing conditions for their crops so in those plants you don't usually see the extremes of form found in harsh conditions. However each fruit and vegetable plant has a certain general form. This form tells us something about which elemental energies predominate in it. When you look at or eat an orange or a pumpkin do you find its bright colour and round shape evokes a feeling of warmth? Warmth energies are needed to produce round shapes and bright colours. Fruits such as oranges and tomatoes need warmth to ripen. Green salad leaves grow in cooler, damp climates: they contain cooler and more watery energies.

Forms of plant and animal species

We cannot attribute all the differences in form we see in plants to environmental influences. Each species has its unique characteristics. Have a good look at some of the vegetables and fruit you eat. Take a carrot. Its bright orange colour and conical form are quite distinctive. We only eat the root, but have you noticed its beautiful feathery leaves? Quite different from the rounded, more watery cabbage leaves. Leek leaves are quite different again. If you start really looking at plants around you, you see that there is a wonderful variety of plants which each have characteristic shapes. There are similar forms that are expressed in a great variety of ways. Looking at deciduous trees in winter, they have beautiful branching forms, each expressing the particular form of their species. Have you thought about how we recognise plants and animals by their characteristic forms?

If a plant or animal does not show the characteristic form for that species we say it is deformed. Most people feel some kind of aversion or pity when they see a deformed plant, animal or human. Why?

Why is this form important? I think it could be because we sense that something has gone wrong, that the plant or animal growth energies are not working in the usual way. When you select fruit and vegetables in the supermarket, I suspect you look for ones with the right form: a lopsided apple or cabbage doesn't look right. It would be interesting to research whether there is any nutritional difference. Form is an important attribute of life.

We are accustomed to attributing all characteristics of living organisms to their genes. Plant seeds carry a blueprint for the plant form in their DNA, but lately scientists have found that the DNA is not as stable as previously thought, it can be modified by environmental influences. We know what genes affect what traits but do we understand what produces the genes? This relates again to the question of how life is produced. The vegetable and grain plants we use for food crops were developed from wild species many centuries ago by people who understood the life energies in plants and how they could be modified.

The German poet and scientist, Johann Wolfgang von Goethe, studied plant forms in a non-judgmental, intuitive and experiential way. In watching how plants develop as they grow from leaves to flowers to seed he evolved his theory of metamorphosis, of the plant's transition from one state to another. Introducing Goethe's book *The Metamorphosis of Plants* (1978, p.15), Rudolf Steiner described Goethe's concept of the archetypal idea of a plant. He said this 'idea' carries the unique energy pattern of that plant. A plant does not remain as one fixed form: it is continually growing and developing, but all the different forms can be seen to evolve out of each other. For example, flower petals look like modified leaves. You might like to try observing a particular plant every day as it grows more leaf after leaf produces flowers and seeds. You may find you enter into a relationship with this unseen essence of the plant.

Goethe believed, like many earlier scientists, that these energy patterns come from energy sources in the wider universe that surrounds our earth. A key concept in Goethe's ideas is that the plant, or any other organism, is not an assembly of cells that work together to form and maintain the whole organism, but it is a whole organism in which some parts are specialised for particular tasks. All parts are maintained by the same basic energy patterns and rhythms.

You can see characteristic forms in insects and animals as well as plants. Have you ever considered how spiders spin such beautiful symmetrical webs and honeybees create hexagonal honeycombs? (See Figure 5.2.) I wonder whether they carry those forms within them or are responding to formative energies around them.

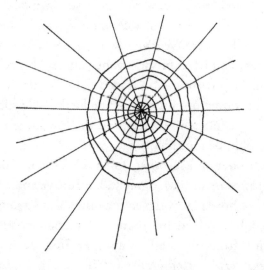

Figure 5.2: Drawing of spider webs and honeycombs.

Rhythmic patterns in water and sound images

I was recently amazed to see pictures of forms very similar to those we see in leaves and flowers and animals that had been produced artificially by sound frequencies. In his book *Water Sound Images* (2006), Alexander Lauterwasser displays many photographs of the geometric patterns formed when sound waves are used to set a steel plate covered by sand into vibration. When a range of sound frequencies were used the patterns changed but continue to be symmetrical and ordered. Such patterns were first demonstrated by Ernst Chladni using a violin bow to stroke the edge of a glass plate covered with a thin layer of sand. Hans Jenny developed this idea using various ways of transmitting sound waves to a steel plate. The sand settles into complex wave patterns. Lauterwasser has shown even more intricate patterns by vibrating the bottom of a container of water. A camera photographs the image made when a light is shone down on the water from above. When there is a regular, consistent impulse which forms waves of a constant wavelength that coincides with the diameter of the container, the water forms 'standing waves' that reflect more light than the troughs in between them, displaying the wave pattern.

Many of the images produced are very similar to the form of a flower or a cross-section through it (see Figure 5.3).

Lauterwasser has also produced patterns very similar to animal forms such as starfish, sea urchin and turtle shells (see Figure 5.4).

If patterns similar to flower forms can be produced by harmonious sound energy vibrations, this suggests to me that flower forms could have been produced in a similar way. Wilhelm Pelikan, in his book *Healing Plants* (1997, p.25) wrote that:

'form derives from the fluid plant nature, which is constantly changing and seen briefly in the physical state'.

Looking at the skin of a new born baby or delicate new green leaves such as of a European beech tree, they are almost translucent – they look as though the physical matter has just appeared in a form that has already been organised by invisible energies As this fluidity hardens into denser matter such as in older people, older leaves and into the bark of trees, it is losing life. This is why it is so beneficial to eat freshly picked, robust plant food such as sprouts and young leaves – they still have plenty of life in them.

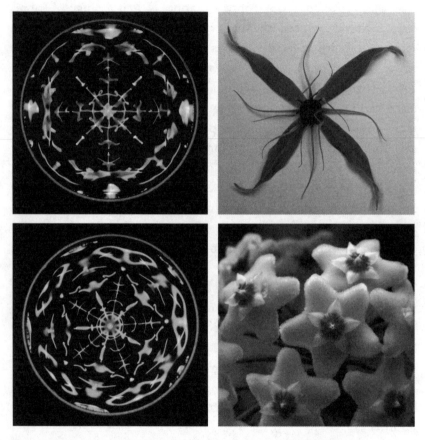

Figure 5.3: Top left: Standing wave photo at 24.24 Hertz showing 4-element structure; top right: Blossom of Paris quadrifolia; *bottom left: Standing wave photo at 38.54 Hertz showing 5-element structure; bottom right: Blossom of wax flower* (Chamelaucium). *From* Water Sound Images *by Alexander Lauterwasser (2006), Macromedia Publishing, USA, p.81, Figures 78–81.*

Figure 5.4: Left: Turtle; right: Chladni sound figures of sand patterns formed by vibrating plate at 1088 Hertz. (top) and 1085 Hertz. (bottom). From Alexander Lauterwasser (2006), p.62, photos 3 and 4.

Quantum science and organising energies in living organisms

Modern science analyses plant parts and constituents. We tend to look at static 'dead' characteristics, but if you look at plant cells under a strong microscope they are streaming – water is constantly taking materials in, out and around cells, just like blood streams around our bodies. Our breathing and our pulses work rhythmically. These are features of living bodies – when they are dead the streaming dries up, the breathing stops. Your body is more than the corpse that is dissected and analysed – it is alive, in constant motion. Chinese have long recognised unseen energies driving the growth and movement in living organisms as 'chi'. Ancient medicine systems such as Chinese medicine, as well as many complementary medicine practitioners, treat the human body as a whole energy system, aiming to restore harmony and balance to this system. The concepts used to describe plants long ago, by investigators such as Hippocrates and Paracelsus, have been replaced by modern scientific analysis. But some of these concepts, which are still the basis for herbal medicine, seem to relate well to the findings of quantum scientists.

Quantum scientists have found that what appears to us as solid matter is actually vibrating energy waves at a quantum level. Can you imagine a plant appearing as the result of the interplay of vibrating energy waves? Biologists are now finding that organisms are more than an assembly of individual cells: they talk about 'dynamic organisation and coherence of biological systems as the synchronisation in space and time through self-organisation' (Lloyd et al p.136). Each organism should be viewed as an integrated whole. David Bohm (1980, p.186) wrote that 'physical law should refer primarily to an order of undivided wholeness of the content of description similar to that indicated by the hologram rather than to an order of analysis of such content into separate parts' .

Energy streams and connectedness also extend beyond individual organisms. When I am completely relaxed and not stressed I feel totally connected and in harmony with everything around me. Many people talk of a similar experience. The biologist Rupert Sheldrake (2009) has said that we are surrounded by resonating 'morphic fields' which have characteristic patterns of activity and structure. These morphic fields have an effect on a whole organism, imposing particular patterns and organisation. Organisms of the same type can tune into their morphic field of collective information, which appear to cover the whole earth and evolve as new information is added. This can explain why the same new behaviour or idea can appear in several different apparently unrelated places at about the same time. Sheldrake has likened such morphic fields to collective memory and habits. He has undertaken various experiments with people that show that our perceptions that seem to be picked up telepathically rather than by usual means of communication can be explained by the presence of resonating morphic fields. The rhythms, structure and DNA of an organism, can also be related to that morphic field or idea, which determines the organisational fields of energy.

Gabriel Cousens, in his book, *Conscious Eating* (2000, pp.275–80) described a similar whole organism organisational effect which he termed: 'Subtle Organising Energy Fields' (SOEFs), He described these fields as templates for physical biological forms and structures.

Rudolf Steiner took a similar wholistic approach to living organisms when he developed the concepts elaborated by Goethe. He looked for a unifying, rhythmic principle in the whole plant, rather than taking it apart and analysing constituents. He observed that plant and animal cells are constantly growing and reproducing. If you chop off a cutting from a plant you can grow a whole new plant from it – the idea of the whole is within the part. Some animals such as earthworms have this ability too, but humans do not. Steiner described the energies that enable living organisms to grow in this way as 'formative forces' (Goethe 1978, pp.16–18). A better term for present day understanding could be 'organisational energies'.

To get an idea of what is meant by formative force or SOEF, have a look at the patterns made by flowing water on the bottom of a stream bed or on the beach. They clearly show some kind of organised pattern. Or look at the meandering course of a natural river bed. Many more natural forms are discussed in a fascinating book by Theodor Schwenk (1965). He studied how water flows in a spiral movement and showed how shells appear to have grown by a similar flowing movement to produce spiral patterns.

We find it hard to believe that something is real when we cannot perceive it with our senses of sight, hearing and touch. However, some people have developed different kinds of senses to 'see' and 'hear' formative energies. They describe this as an awe-inspiring experience. Dorian Schmidt (2005) has described many different dynamic forces around plants, with different ones for each plant species.

According to Steiner, each plant idea is a result of particular formative forces or energies, which can be reinforced if the plant is 'in tune with' its immediate environment and the wider environment of planets and stars (1993, pp.20, 262). The formative energies in these plants are constantly and rhythmically circulating in them.

Rhythm and form in living organisms

What evidence can we find to back up Steiner's assertion that plants relate to planets and stars? Many examples have been shown of how animal and plant forms and behaviours relate to moon rhythms (Endres & Schad 2002). This is seen particularly in sea organisms such as corals and squid that relate to tidal rhythms, but also in land organisms. Scientists have found that every living organism has a sequence of many interlinked rhythms, connected with those of its environment in time and space. Examples in humans include nerve action, heartbeat, peristalsis, sleep/waking, menstruation and activity of the organs. Such rhythms are linked to lunar rhythms but are also independent, regulated by our own bodies.

If living organisms are affected by rhythms from the moon orbiting the earth, then it seems quite possible that they are also affected by rhythms from other orbiting planetary bodies. Ernst Kranich (1986) describes many patterns seen in plants that correspond to the movement of planets around the earth (see Figure 5.5). As seen from the earth, the planets make quite complex patterns while orbiting around the sun. For example, in eight years the movement of the planet Venus round the earth describes a pentagon pattern very similar to the pattern of the petals of the rose, buttercup and many other flowers. Mercury's movement around the sun is reflected in the pattern of leaf shoot development – particularly in monocotyledon plants such as onions. It also relates to the three or six petalled flower structure of plants such as lilies and roses.

Relating plants to the planets is not a new idea: Nicholas Culpeper's complete herbal book written in the seventeenth

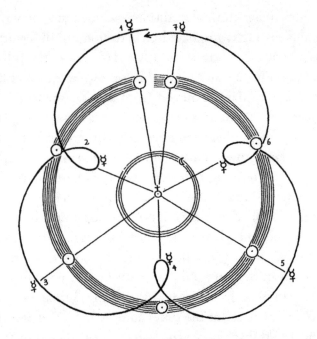

Figure 5.5: Diagram showing how the planet Mercury, as seen from the earth, circles around the Sun about three times in one year. At three or four times during the year Mercury is in line with and behind the Sun (1,3,5,7) and at three times during the year Mercury is in front of the sun (2,4,6). From Planetary Influences upon Plants *by Ernst Kranich (1986), Biodynamic Literature, USA, p.21, Figure 3.*

century describes each herb as being governed by a particular planet (Culpeper 1995). Astronomers have based much of their knowledge about stars and planets on analysis of the radio waves they emit and which are picked up by radio telescopes on earth: for example, Jupiter sends out particularly strong radio waves. Can you entertain the idea that plants respond to finer energy signals from the universe beyond our earth? I believe we have a lot more learning to do before we really understand the incredible life processes in plants and animals that we generally take for granted. Observation of how whole plants grow with appreciation and respect is likely to be more helpful for this understanding than microscopic analysis of plant chemistry and biology.

Many ancient agricultural traditions include times favourable for planting and sowing crops, based on astronomical observations. A common practice is to sow seeds a few days before the full moon, when the moon has a watery influence on the earth, which favours seed germination. Maria Thun in Germany has spent many years sowing seeds at different times and recording where planetary positions are at those times, and how the plants grew. She found clear patterns in plant growth characteristics such as stem length, root length, time of flowering that correspond to particular planetary configurations and rhythms (Thun 2003, pp.13–19).

It seems possible that plants' DNA organisational blueprint for protein is reinforced when plants 'hear' the right tone energy for their species. This energy could come from a source or a particular mix of sources in the stars and planets. It may be possible in future to reproduce this energy ourselves. In 1994 the journal *New Scientist* published an article about the tunes composed by Joel Sternheimer (Coghland 1994). Each note was chosen to correspond to an amino acid in a protein, with the full tune corresponding to the entire protein. What this means is that the sounds sequenced in just the right order results in a tune which is unique and harmonises with the internal structure of a specific plant type. According to *New Scientist,* 'Sternheimer claims that each plant type has a different sequence of notes to stimulate its growth. When plants "hear" the appropriate tune, they produce more of that protein. He also writes tunes that inhibit the synthesis of proteins'. In other words, desirable plants could be stimulated to grow while undesirable plants (weeds for instance) could be inhibited. This is done with electromagnetic energy, in this case sound waves, pulsed to the right set of frequencies thus affecting the plant at an energetic and submolecular level.

Some years ago a product called 'Sonic Bloom' was bought by some New Zealand orchardists to increase fruit production. It played sound tones to mimic birdsong, giving signals to plant leaves to take in more carbon dioxide and liquid fertiliser. This stimulating effect on plant growth must also result from real birdsong. I find their song also has a harmonising effect. Some farmers find that playing harmonious music to their cows during milking time increases milk yield. Possibly birdsong and music are also affecting the quality of food produced.

The 'music of the spheres'

When we go about our daily lives on earth it's hard to comprehend that we are living on an earth that is spinning rapidly around itself and around the sun, surrounded by planets and galaxies that are also spinning around. All this movement generates energy fields. Pythagoras and his disciples related musical tones to the constantly moving ratios of planetary orbits to each other and found a wonderful harmony in these movements. They described the generally unheard sounds emanating from the universe around us as the 'Music of the Spheres'. In the early seventeenth century Johannes Kepler used mathematics to study planetary motions to build on this idea, relating the harmony of musical ratios to planetary velocities, the time it takes to complete an orbit and their distance from the Sun.

When I see the beauty and diversity of all the plant forms around me in my garden, and then the incredible number of stars in the sky at night, I feel that there is still so much to understand about the beautiful world we live in. Looking at Lauterwasser's sound music pictures (Lauterwasser 2006) I am reminded of the words at the beginning of St John's Gospel about the creative Word of God: 'In the beginning was the Word, and the Word was with God and the Word was God ... All things were made by him.' (King James Bible 1769).

This suggests to me a picture of the Creative Word, creating music of the universe, which plays through the circling of the planets and stars, sending out repetitive rhythmic, harmonic waves. Astrologers such as Glen Atkinson (1989) describe how these waves intermingle and resonate with each other, setting up patterns which are taken up by water and elements around our earth, forming the living plants and animals we see. It appears that the many similar basic forms in our plants and animals are connected in some way with energy from our wider universe. There is increasing evidence that the living organisms on our earth are built from energy rhythms.

Projective geometry and ether energies

Plants growing vigorously in spring have a wonderful glow around them, shooting upwards and outwards. Have you ever wondered how they defy gravity, as though they are pulled up by invisible strings? In Goethe's study of plants (1978, p.18) he found that plants grow through alternate expansion and contraction. Life, and growth, depend on the interplay between opposing energy forces. Plants respond to unseen energies in our earth atmosphere and in the surrounding universe.

Unseen, unmeasurable energies can be explained by the mathematics of projective geometry, which relates points and planes. George Adams and Olive Whicher (1980) have used this form of geometry to explain how plants respond to opposing unseen forces in their growth and development. The growth forces pushing them up from the earth are met by forces streaming in from the universe around the earth. These concepts are very important for a real understanding of how plants grow.

Rudolf Steiner termed some of these unseen energies 'ethers'. He described life, light, warmth and tone ethers, as being subtle energies that work in the opposite way to the elements, earth, air, fire and water. Etheric energy can be thought of as negative energy. These ethers cannot be detected by our senses, but we can see their effects in the world around us. For example, Ernst Marti describes how light ether makes things visible, and tone ether separates things into organised patterns (Marti 1984, pp.19, 23). The sound water pictures described above would be produced by tone ether.

The effects of these elements and ethers and their interactions can be seen in plant forms. A plant with a lot of fire and warmth influence tends to have rounded leaves and flowers and fruits with warm colours, such as pumpkins and melons. Plants in which the water and tone influence predominates, such as mint, grow best in moist places, producing lush growth with half-moon shaped leaves. The earth and life influence produces aromatic plants with square stems such as mints and lavender, while light and airy plants, such as carrots and flaxes, have more indented, spiky leaves. I frequently marvel at the wonderful feeling of energy and movement amongst carrot leaves, and even more so among the leaves of fennel, which comes from the same plant family, Umbelliferae. They give a wonderful sensation of the intermingling and weaving together of light and air and water and warmth which produce the root we eat as carrot.

Energies from the surrounding universe stimulate formative forces in the ethers to form the physical plant forms we see (Marti 1984, p.8). The plant form is continually maintained by internalised formative energies that form what Steiner termed their 'etheric bodies'. He said that animals and humans also have etheric bodies of flowing energies that keep their physical bodies alive and prevent decay (Steiner 1972, pp.23, 24). As with plants, these etheric bodies are maintained by formative forces flowing in from the cosmos around us (Steiner 1921). Animals and humans also have what Steiner termed 'astral bodies' which are maintained by a different kind of energy that enables them to feel, move and be conscious. Some healers, such as Barbara Ann Brennan see these energy bodies as 'auras' and can describe them (Brennan 1987). She can observe seven aura layers around people, looking 'as if they are composed of strings of many tiny, rapidly blinking lights, each blinking at a different rate'. Steiner (1972, p.28–34) also describes a further body, the ego body, which is only in humans and enables us to think and have memory of past experiences.

This all suggests to me a wonderful picture of life as vibrating energy rhythms, Each plant and animal is like a musical tune which is pleasing and uplifting when the individual notes are harmonised together in a particular rhythm. We are a wonderful creation of resonating, harmonious rhythm. If we humans and all organisms are whole beings, resonating in harmony with other organisms and the whole universe around us, rather than an assembly of cells, genes and biochemicals, then we need to look at the food we eat in relation to its whole integrity rather than its content of nutrients.

The way plants are grown, and their relationship to their environment, could have considerable effects on the amount of organisational energy they contain. If all the four types of energy, warmth, light, tone and life, need to be interacting harmoniously in the plant, then this is an important task for gardeners to aim for this to happen. Similarly, the value of animal food products would depend on how much organisational energies are in the food the animals ate. This could be why the eggs from chickens that range freely on growing pasture, exposed to sunlight, taste so much better than eggs from battery hens. We need to develop a better understanding of life before our analytical thinking and our consumption of 'fake' food compromise the life that supports us.

PART 2.

NUTRITION FOR BODY, SOUL AND SPIRIT

6. Vitamins, Phytonutrients and Minerals

We are used to thinking of our nutrition requirements in terms of so many calories, or the minimum quantity of a nutrient recommended for the average person to keep healthy, such as minerals and vitamins and possibly also in terms of Omega oils and protein contents. In the UK this is known as the Recommended Daily Allowance (RDA), in the USA as Recommended Daily Intake (RDI), or Nutrient Reference Values (NRVs) in Australia and New Zealand. RDA guides are only approximate, as each individual person needs different quantities according to their age and lifestyle, individual metabolism, their digestive ability and how well they absorb nutrients. However, these values are based on a lot of careful research and they serve as very useful guides in designing diets and correcting nutrient deficiencies. In this chapter I focus particularly on vitamins and phytonutrients.

Vitamin requirements and supplements

We all know that vitamins are important for our health, but are we getting enough? The debate about whether or not to take vitamin supplements in addition to eating fruit and vegetables is confusing. Patrick Holford (2004, p.105) points out that there is a large variation in vitamin content of fruit and vegetables on the market. Many bought vegetables contain low levels of vitamins, particularly if they have been stored for a while. He recommends taking vitamin supplements, and refers to studies that show that high levels of vitamins are needed for optimum health (Cheraskin *et al.* 1994). These recommended levels are often at least ten times as much as the Recommended Daily Allowance (RDA).

For example, Holford recommends 2000 mg vitamin C per day. The UK RDA for healthy adults of vitamin C is 50 mg/day (UK) and in New Zealand and Australia the Nutrient Reference Values (NRVs) give a greater range of recommendations according to age, sex, pregnancy, and so on, but for 97–98% of healthy adults the recommended daily intake is 45 mg/day. Holford points out that to obtain 2000 mg vitamin C one would have to eat forty-four average oranges.

For the other side of the argument, a fact-sheet recently put on the internet by the University of Colorado states that: 'Vitamin deficiency is rare unless a person's diet is limited and lacks variety' (Anderson & Roach 2010). And observes that much of the over $23.7 billion a year spent on supplements in the USA are wasted as they are not absorbed by the body. It also states that: 'Very high doses of many vitamins such as A, C, D and B-6, as well as several minerals, can cause serious health problems if taken regularly.' For example, consumption of high levels of b-carotene was linked to an increase in death from lung cancer.

The questions of how much is needed and in what form is important now that more and more nutrients are being added to our food to ensure everyone gets enough. If a child eats a lot of a particular nutrient fortified food there is a danger they could eat too much of a nutrient. A key consideration is one's state of health. If the body is sick often there is poor absorption and assimilation of nutrients so vitamin supplements may be needed. Doctors have found that large doses of vitamin pills can help in healing disease. A recent story on New Zealand TV showed a man with swine flu, expected to die from severe lung congestion, who recovered after being given very high doses of vitamin C. High doses of vitamins have been helpful in overcoming conditions such as cancer. People with chronic disease conditions or with food digestion and absorption difficulties may need higher vitamin doses than those who are healthier.

Further difficulties in prescribing daily nutrient intake levels arise from the large variation between abilities of different people to digest and absorb nutrients and from what combination of nutrients are eaten at a particular time. Some nutrients inhibit absorption of other nutrients. Some scientists recognise that vitamins are more easily absorbed and more beneficial when they are eaten in whole fruit and vegetables rather than in pills (Shayne, 2000).

Efficacy of vitamin pills in overcoming disease does not necessarily mean that healthy people need to consume such pills in order to keep healthy. Such an approach would follow on from a concept of the human body as a machine which needs a certain quantity and quality of food (fuel) to keep it healthy. We are not just machines, nor an assembly of chemicals that needs to be topped up with all the right chemical nutrients. We are alive. The concept of life being maintained by unseen organisational energies, discussed in the previous two chapters, applies to humans as well as plants.

Our bodies as living, integrated systems

Observation that the same diet has very different effects in different people shows that our bodies are more complex than machines. Rather than focusing on the many complex chemical reactions going on in all our cells and the nutrients involved in them, can we visualise our bodies as whole systems, functioning through integrated energy flows? If particular energies get too strong or too weak the body gets out of balance and gets sick. Or it may get overwhelmed by strong energies from outside.

Formative forces and nutrition

When we think about our bodies as living energy systems then it follows that the food we eat can affect the energy organisation of our bodies. Food value depends on its 'inner quality' and coherence. The nutrient content and material substance is less important than the life processes or organisational energies in the food. The most important requirement for food is that it be alive, with strong formative forces or organisational energies. To grow food of good nutritional quality, of the right 'energetic state', the plants and animals and the soil they are grown in have to be nourished by living substances (Steiner 1994, p.69).

Even though the formative energies in a food are more important for our nutrition than the chemical constituents of that food, it is important that these constituents are present in suitable quantities in the food. The plant or animal that produces the food needs to have all these nutrients present and in the right balance to be healthy with strong formative energies. Proteins, oils and carbohydrates are important for nourishment of particular parts and energies of our bodies.

So what are vitamins?

How can vitamins be related to this concept of formative forces or organisational energies? Biochemists isolated chemicals which they called vitamins and these chemicals can be formulated in the laboratory for making vitamin supplements. But it is not so simple as that. For example, ascorbic acid is generally taken for vitamin C. But when foods are analysed for vitamin C content, the content of the dehydroascorbic acid form has to be measured as well as there is constant conversion from one chemical to another. The chemical analysis of foods has been useful but has led to our focus on specific nutrients, which can be supplied in supplements if there is not enough in our food.

If we start to think in terms of whole plants and organisational energies rather than chemicals, we get a whole different picture. Although ascorbic acid pills can overcome the disease symptoms of vitamin C deficiency, ascorbic acid may only be the end result of a whole process in the human body. Vitamin C is highly reactive. This is a characteristic of all vitamins – they assist chemical reactions, like enzymes. Vitamins act as regulators of many metabolic activities.

For example, vitamin D regulates calcium and phosphorus levels in the blood. Only small quantities are needed to do this. So it makes sense to me to think of them as processes of energy rather than as the complex chemical formulae of the chemicals they produce. Rather than depending on a chemical to prevent disease symptoms, it would be better to find foods that provide the energies of the vitamin processes.

We can understand vitamins better by thinking about deficiency symptoms, what the vitamin does in the body and where they are found in food. For example scurvy, in which the skin breaks down and bleeds, can be cured by large doses of vitamin C. One of the main functions of vitamin C in the body is as an antioxidant. It takes up the free oxygen that is produced through energy transfer in the body, preventing oxidation chain reactions which result in damaged cells. The best sources of vitamin C are fresh plant leaves and fruit. The growing of plant leaves and fruit requires them to take in and process light. Research has shown that light has a direct effect on vitamin C (ascorbic acid) content, which increased in crops up to 800% higher with increasing light intensity (Somers & Beeson 1948). Bright green leaves contain vitamin C and therefore light activity. Light in excess can often bring about oxidation and breakdown of living tissues. As the vitamin C process seems to relate to light, does light energy generate vitamin C? In his book *Nutrition*, Rudolf Hauschka (2002, p.127) drew this conclusion and he similarly related the other main vitamins to the other ether energies I discussed in Chapter 5.

Hauschka said that as vitamin A is particularly found in animal fats, fruits, oily seeds, green leaves and roots such as carrots, which all need warmth to develop, and its deficiency causes stunting, poor vision and poor immunity, it relates to the warmth energy or ether. B vitamins are concentrated in fruit skins, grain husks and green leaves. Their deficiency symptoms include muscle wasting and disorders of the nervous and cardiovascular systems. Hauschka considered that this indicates a relationship to enclosing and ordering, chemical forming energies which are provided by musical tones and the tone ether. Children with vitamin D deficiency are unable to form bone properly and the best source of vitamin D is fish oils, particularly deep sea fish. In the dark sea depths where light does not penetrate, the mineralising, crystallising, forming powers of earth energies or 'life ether' are likely to have greatest effect.

Such possible connections between ether energies and the vitamins need to be investigated. I suspect the relationships are more complex than Hauschka thought, that the effects of the vitamins in the body are a result of interactions between two or more ether energies. This could explain why many more vitamins have been isolated, such as all the different B vitamins. Each could relate to a particular combination of ether energies. Possibly it is interactions between ether energies and mineral element energies that generate vitamins. Relationships between vitamins and minerals are common, for example vitamin E and selenium work together and cobalt is needed for vitamin B12. This is speculation, but I would like to see scientists looking at whole energy processes and effects rather than analysing chemicals.

However they are produced, I think it safe to conclude that the best sources of vitamins are the foods they are contained in, remembering that the content varies a lot according to how the foods are grown, how fresh they are and how much has been lost in cooking.

Returning to the debate about quantities of vitamins to take, I wonder whether the lower figure of official recommendations is correct if the vitamin is consumed in its natural state, as part of 'alive' food. The higher figure recommended by Holford may be what is needed if manufactured vitamin pills are taken. It is likely that the more vitamin pills you consume, the less the body is able to use the vitamin process through food digestion. The vitamin in live food would act as a stimulant for the recipient body to develop its own rhythmic energies to perform the functions that the vitamin supports. The manufactured vitamin, on the other hand, would not have this stimulating effect, it just supplies a chemical that is involved in the process so would continually need to be replenished to perform those functions. Or maybe the difference is like the difference between allopathic and homeopathic medicines. The latter are more effective in smaller concentrations because they are working on an energetic rather than a chemical level.

Phytonutrients

A large range of chemicals that are beneficial to our health have been discovered in plants. They have been termed phytonutrients or phytochemicals. Some act as antioxidants, some stabilise hormones and some stimulate the immune system. Examples are glucosinolates in broccoli and other Brassica or Cruciferae vegetables, and allium compounds in onions and garlic, which have various anti-carcinogenic actions. It seems likely that these chemicals result from interaction of formative energies in the plant, in a similar way to vitamins. As with the vitamins, it is likely that it is the living energy itself that is most beneficial, rather than the chemical end-product. It is best to eat these phytochemicals within whole fruit and vegetables as part of a whole mixed diet rather than as isolated chemicals.

Minerals

Many minerals and trace minerals are needed for nutrition but because people have different digestive capacities and the mineral content of foods is so variable, it is difficult to determine exactly how much minerals are in our food and what each person needs. As with other nutrients, it is helpful to think of mineral nutrients in terms of their energy processes. Most minerals enable activities in the body that are repeated over and over again, so only small quantities are needed. Trace elements are involved in enzyme and vitamin activities. Minerals such as magnesium, sodium, potassium and phosphorus are involved in cell physiological processes, maintaining healthy life processes, and phosphorus and many trace elements with energy processes.

It is the activity of these minerals that is important. The mineral that is extracted from food and measured is the end result of this activity process. When the mineral consumed is part of a living plant or animal product, it can be more readily digested and used in the human body.

It is so easy to forget that the food we eat originates in living plants and animals. When I harvest fruit and vegetables from the plants that grew them, I feel very thankful to these plants that have grown to provide good food.

7. How Formative Energies Affect Digestion and Nutrition

The basic processes of digestion we learned about in biology classes did not seem very exciting, but if you think about it in an imaginative way it is an awe-inspiring process. Our digestive organs recognise what we eat and secrete the right enzymes to digest all the different components of the meal. This enables us to eat a large variety of foods and use them to give us energy and to grow our bodies.

Digestion and assimilation

The taste and aroma of food stimulate our metabolic organs to secrete enzymes to help digest it. Carbohydrates, fats and oils, protein and minerals all go through different digestion processes as they are broken down. Our bodies accomplish a great number of energy transformations in digestion, keeping us alive, healthy and active.

Digestion breaks down food into its chemical components so it can be built up again into our own bodies. Not only the chemicals, but also the organisational energies that we take in have to be destroyed and in that process, stimulate our own organisational energies which use the nutrients. Our bodies are not machines but dynamic, living and self-organising. They need more than so many calories and so many grams of various chemicals. We need the stimulation of rhythmical organisational energies in our food to maintain the rhythms and harmony of our organs, our circulating blood, our breathing, our energy cycles, our immune systems, our thinking and feeling. Eugen Kolisko (1978, p.9) pointed out that all substances have to be transformed into substances which can exist in human blood. He gave a detailed description of the digestive processes.

The energy pattern and rhythm in each piece of food we eat is foreign to our own body and cannot be assimilated and used in that form. Food has to be completely broken down by our digestive enzymes then assimilated and built up again into our own energy rhythms and our own unique proteins. When protein is digested it is broken down into its constituent parts, then the body uses the formative energy released to builds up its own protein. A protein molecule is a highly organised structure of amino acids which themselves are complex organised molecules. The blueprint or energy pattern of each amino acid is needed to enable us to rebuild them after completely breaking them down by digestion. Steiner said that our bodies do not retain those blueprints, they need to be provided each day for us to be able to build our own protein (Steiner 1991, p.112). Each human makes their own unique protein – that is why DNA sampling can be used for identification at a crime scene. We particularly need the blueprint structure of each of these substances, particularly complex proteins,

Our bodies can only build healthy protein if we eat balanced protein foods containing all the essential amino acids. Plant protein is particularly important. The smaller quantity of protein in plant foods compared to in animal foods provides more stimulation of our own energies because plant proteins are harder to digest. Animal protein is more similar to our own protein than is plant protein.

Everyone has a unique digestive system, digesting these various types of substance differently. Some people are better able to digest food than others, depending on such factors as the health of their digestive organs and their psychological state. Wolcott and Fahey (2000) described many types of imbalance such as the rate of food oxidation, electrolyte/fluid balance and dominance of an endocrine gland, all of which can affect digestion and which vary between each person. Good feeding and care of babies and young children helps to build healthy digestive organs which can contribute to health in later life.

The rate at which we metabolise glucose has considerable affects not only on cellular functions and physical energy but also on our state of mind. George Watson (1972)ʹ categorised people into slow and fast glucose oxidisers, finding relationships between this metabolism rate and mental disorders. He found that fast oxidisers needed a different diet to improve their condition than that which benefited slow oxidisers. He also found that lack of particular vitamins could affect people psychologically, and also could affect their sense of smell.

The interconnections between our minds and our digestions is a further reason why each person digests the same food differently. Dr Edward Bach found a relationship between the predominant species of bacteria in a person's gut and their basic attitude to life (Howard, 1990, p.7). Someone who is fearful has different gut bacteria to someone who is more relaxed and is enjoying life.

Our gut bacteria play a major role in digestion and assimilation. Scientists at the Institute of Food Research, UK, estimate there are about ten trillion microbial cells living in the human gut (Juge *et al.* n.d.).

Eating food in a fresh, natural state such as raw milk and yogurt and fresh salads assists with keeping healthy gut bacteria which protect against harmful bacteria.

With so many different factors affecting our digestion and assimilation of food it is no wonder that particular diets have different effects on different people. Chronic disease states such as leaky gut syndrome further complicate food assimilation. An unsuitable diet is unhelpful no matter how good quality the food is. This is why we all need to take responsibility for our own nutrition and health. Learning to be aware of the taste, smell and appearance of different foods and how they affect your energy levels and state of mind helps to build consciousness, both directly and through selecting the right, high quality food.

Relationships between plant and human energies

When you eat your five servings of fruit and vegetables a day, do you think about what types of fruit and vegetables? Generally we take into account whether they are starchy or contain more protein, trace elements, other nutrients and antioxidants. Also important is the question of what kind of fruit, vegetable or animal food. When formative forces are considered it could make a difference whether I eat an apple or a pear or a carrot as they each have different combinations of formative energies and rhythms. A leafy vegetable such as lettuce contains different energies from a root vegetable such as carrots. A broccoli head is actually a plant flower, so this contains different energies again.

When you eat an apple you eat the energy processes that were used by the apple and the tree it grew on to maintain life. When the apple that has been broken down by digestion is assimilated by your body, these energies stimulate your own energy processes. In earlier times people considered the whole plant or animal food rather than its constituents. The idea that a plant form can resemble part of a human body, indicating that it can be used to heal that part is generally dismissed as unscientific. It was a very ancient belief revived in the sixteenth century by Paracelsus as the 'doctrine of signatures' and also used in Chinese traditional medicine. There are some remarkable similarities often quoted such as that walnuts look like a brain and are good for brain function, and the lungwort plant is helpful in healing lungs.

Effects of eating different types of plant energy

Paracelsus and other alchemists identified three main types of energy, which they called 'Salt', 'Mercury' and 'Sulphur'. Salt energies produce mineral salt forms. These energies are predominant in plant roots. Sulphur energies enable warm, metabolic, differentiating processes in plants, resulting in flowers and seeds. The mercurial energy refers to the flowing and rhythmic nature of all liquids, which flow between the salt and sulphur extremes. Mercury energies predominate in plant leaves.

Rudolf Steiner related different parts of the plant and their processes to different parts of the human body (Steiner 1991, pp.98, 106). He said that these relationships are the basis of how different parts of the plant have different nutritional effects in the body. Eating particular parts of the plant stimulates and nourishes corresponding parts of our body. Steiner visualised the plant as an upside down human. The roots correspond to our heads – the mineral energies in the soil which are taken up by roots are similar to the energies in our heads and nervous system. The leaves relate to our respiratory and circulatory systems and the flowers, fruit and seeds to our digestive system and limbs.

When you follow through this concept into nutrition, it becomes apparent that it could make a difference which part of a vegetable you eat. Steiner said that eating root vegetables such as carrots and beetroot can help the thinking, nerve based processes concentrated in our heads, leaves are beneficial for lungs and blood circulation and flowers and fruit for digestion. He further elaborated how this approach could be used to feed animals appropriate food according to whether they are to produce milk, be fattened or for growing calves (Steiner 1993, p.159–66). For example, feeding calves root vegetables, which contain a lot of mineral salts, enables them to develop their nerves and senses in a healthy way. I have not found any modern research that backs up this theory, although a specialist in nutrition science might find some. There is some evidence from traditional practices. For example, chamomile flowers, fruit and fennel seeds are commonly used to help digestion. You might like to experiment with your diet to see if you find any difference from eating these various parts of the plant.

Some scientists did investigate Steiner's ideas in the early twentieth century, using different methodology from that now required. Eugen Kolisko, a doctor who undertook extensive research, said that the various formative energies in plants are rhythmical and affect the rhythmical processes of the human body (Kolisko 1978, p.30). He found that the blood circulation and its transport of sugar, starch and minerals around the body are particularly affected by the energy rhythms. When you eat fruits they stimulate the rhythms of the digestive system. He said that eating processed sugar has a quite different effect from the sugar in fruits, because it is inert, no longer living. Similarly, the mineral salts in root vegetables stimulate our nerves, consciousness and thinking, but eating a mineral salt such as dolomite does not have that effect.

These concepts could provide an important reason why some people have found a wholefood diet to be beneficial. The nutrients in processed foods may appear to be the same, but they are not, as they do not carry energy rhythms. Bread is made from flour which would lose much of its energies in the milling process. Eating cooked whole grains, which retain these energies, would stimulate the metabolism and limbs, our 'doing' energy. Eating fresh green salads stimulates our breathing and blood circulation, keeping us alive and healthy. Root vegetables contain a lot of minerals drawn from the earth. Eating them provides these minerals in a living, dynamic form to stimulate our thinking, our consciousness of who we are. Eating mineral supplements would not have this energetic effect.

The energies in foods can affect not only our physical health but our feelings and behaviour. Maria Geuter, in the introduction to her book, *Herbs in Nutrition* (1962), describes how children can be assisted to develop more rounded temperaments, through eating particular vegetables and herbs. For example a forceful and overactive 'choleric' child can be more amenable if they eat plenty of starchy food and root vegetables. Those foods would accentuate the inactivity and lethargy of a 'phlegmatic' child. That child needs a good variety of food including plenty of fresh salads and fruit.

Have you noticed that people living in different areas, on different soils tend to have different physique? I have observed that people born and brought up on clay plains tend to be shorter and stockier than those on sandy areas. I wonder how much this reflects the earth energies in that area and how much the energies in the locally grown food. I recently travelled from New Zealand to England and noticed a difference in the vegetables there – they were thicker, chunkier, more dense, particularly the lettuces. I needed to eat less than in New Zealand. I wondered what caused this difference, whether it was an effect of less light and more earth energies in England, compared to New Zealand. If vegetables grown in different areas have different nutritional effects, this is a factor relevant to the debate about the benefits of eating locally grown food.

Pictorial quality assessment of plant formative forces

As formative forces in plants cannot be measured in the usual way we need more imaginative ways of assessment. Ehrenfried Pfeiffer (1984) developed a method of showing the formative force content of a plant pictorially by the sensitive crystallisation method . Have you ever noticed the patterns made by hoar frost on window panes? The crystallisation method is similar. Plant sap is added to copper chloride solution and a thin layer is poured on to a glass plate. The plate is kept absolutely still in a chamber designed to eliminate any movement, until the liquid all evaporates, leaving crystals. These crystals are formed in a definite pattern that can be related to the health of the plant and the way it has been grown.

Each plant forms a characteristic pattern of crystals. The method is used quite frequently in Europe to assess food quality. It is also used with human blood and urine to assess health conditions and with animal products such as milk. Dr Ursula Balzer-Graf (1999) claims to tell with 99% accuracy whether milk has been pasteurised or not and whether it comes from a cow on a biodynamic farm or not.

Christian Marcel used this methodology to assess the quality of wines. He was able to show clear differences between different soil types, between wines grown on different soil-types. A further set of pictures showed how well the vines producing the wine-grapes had adapted to the soil and environment (see Figure 7.1). The structure and texture of the crystals provide an indication of the energies in the test material. He emphasised that interpretation of these pictures requires a lot of experience.

An understanding of the formative energies in plants could become an important scientific tool in the future for plant breeders as well as nutritionists. In the following chapter I discuss how observation of formative energies in food plants can be used to indicate their nutritional value.

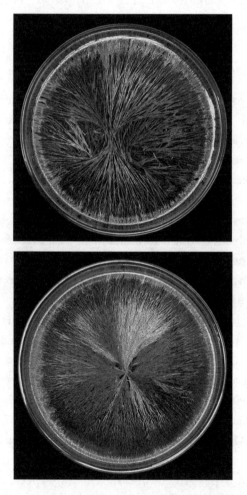

Figure 7.1: Sensitive crystallisation pictures showing champagne made from grapes. Top: under intensive management; and bottom: under biodynamic management. From Marcel, Sensitive Crystallization *(2011), Floris Books, pp. 50, 51, Figures 21, 22.*

8. Formative Energies in some Common Foods

We generally take for granted the wonderful gift of our food plants, that bring together the elements and energies from the sun and air, water and earth to nourish us. The vegetable plants that we grow and eat were developed from wild plants long ago. The early gardeners used their perception of the energies in the plants and developed techniques to enhance particular energies so that larger roots or leaves or fruits were developed. Plant breeders have selected for particular traits over hundreds of years since then, developing many different varieties, but the basic types of vegetable remain the same.

In this chapter we consider how the forms of some common vegetable and other food plants could indicate their nutritional value. I have drawn on the detailed observations of plant families and the forms of healing herbs described by Wilhelm Pelikan in his book, *Healing Plants* (1997) and by Eugen Kolisko in his lectures on nutrition (1978). Although we do not generally look for healing from our food in the same way as herbs are used in healing, it could be helpful to eat particular types of food to help maintain health.

Pelikan's and Kolisko's descriptions show that the way two or more types of formative energy interact with each other; how they combine together or oppose each other in a plant, determines their effect when eaten or used as a medicine. Many of the healing herbs show particularly dominating effects of one type of energy, which makes them useful in healing a particular disease condition. Generally, for nutrition, a balanced interplay of energies in the plant food is desirable. Such balance and harmony are sought when interpreting the formative energy effects in the crystallisation pictures referred to in Chapter 7.

I find that when I think about the vegetable or other food I am eating and about how it grows, I appreciate and enjoy it more. As I observe more and respect the food plants and the energies that enable them to grow I feel that they seem to nourish me more. Many of us have lost that connection with our food plants and the land they grow in, which may have more influence on our nutrition than we realise.

Carrots

We are most familiar with carrots as a long, tapered root, bright orange in colour, although there are purple and yellow varieties. The original carrots are likely to have had purple or yellow roots: the modern orange carrot was developed and stabilised by Dutch growers in the sixteenth and seventeenth centuries. When you cut a carrot horizontally you see a beautiful regular pattern (see Figure 8.1).

The colour and shape of the root, and the very fine, divided and indented leaves and thin, ribbed stems, all indicate a strong predominance of light energies. Pelikan (1997, p.57) describes how in leaves of the carrot plant family, air and water, light and dark all interact and the resulting substance streams down into the roots. In most plants the light energies do not work right down into the roots so strongly as in the carrot family. Carrots (*Daucus carota*) belong to the large plant family, Umbelliferae which include fennel and parsley. In all these plants the roots store sugar and minerals from the first year of growth, which are then used up the following year to produce flowers and seeds.

Pelikan (1997, p.4) discusses how plant roots are similar to the human head, nerves and senses in that they all have strong mineralising, solidifying processes, but opposite in that the head defies gravity whereas roots grow in the same direction as gravity. If you follow the idea that eating a particular part of a plant has greatest influence on the corresponding part of a human, one would expect that eating carrots would bring strong earthly and light organisational energies into the human head, nervous and sensory systems. The common belief that carrots help you to see in the dark backs up this idea, although this effect is generally related to their high level of carotenoids which are the basis of vitamin A, needed for night vision. However, the carotenoids could be produced by the light energies. Rudolf Steiner (1991, pp.99, 100) said that eating carrots provides strong earth and light energies that stimulate thinking and also work into the intestines, helping to evacuate intestinal worms.

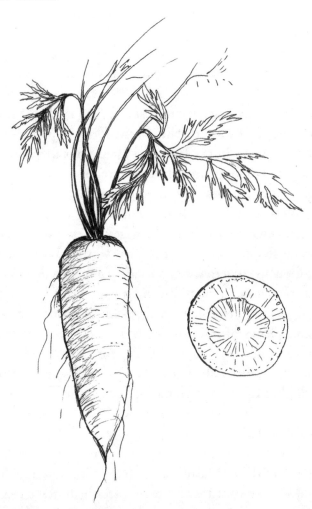

Figure 8.1: Drawings of a carrot plant and its cross-section.

Beetroot

Beetroot (*Beta vulgaris*) is another common root vegetable which is interesting to compare with carrot. It too has a swollen, coloured root, but of a different, round shape. The leaves are also quite different, being larger, rounded, smooth and fleshy. This indicates that there is less light energy and more watery energy that has combined with the strong mineral earth energy. Beetroot's dark red colour also indicates warmth drawn into the swollen root. The whole plant seems more watery and rounded compared to the dryer, lighter carrot plant.

Pelikan (1997, p.204) says that in beetroot the sugar processes are brought under the control of salt processes in the root, so eating it will help bring the digestive processes more strongly under the control of the organising head forces. Kolisko (1978, p.44) explains this process a bit further: that the sugar forming process which in most plants happens in the fruit and affects our metabolic system when eaten, is working strongly in the roots. Because eating roots mainly affects our nervous system, eating beetroot stimulates the part of the nervous system that works in the metabolism. One effect of these strong organisational energies in the digestive system is that eating raw beetroot helps to control intestinal worms. Beetroot has also been traditionally used to treat a variety of ailments including fevers and illnesses relating to digestion and the blood.

Because the mineralising energies in beetroot are strong it accumulates plenty of minerals, so is a good source of potassium, magnesium, iron, zinc, calcium, phosphorus, and sodium. These mineral levels are generally higher than in carrots, and beetroot also contains higher levels of B vitamins, but less carotene, vitamins E and K than carrots. However, as pointed out in Chapter 3, these levels are calculated as average values and can vary considerably.

Beetroot has been found to have an extremely low GL (Glycemic Load) of 2.9, in spite of having a 'medium' GI (Glycemic Index) of 64. The low GL means that beetroot carbohydrates are converted into sugars very slowly, helping to keep blood sugar levels stable.

Possibly this feature of sugar regulation is related to the organisation of the sugar processes in the growing root mentioned by Pelikan.

Potatoes

In contrast to beetroot, potatoes have a high glycemic index. They contain a large quantity of starch which is converted quickly to sugar. Rudolf Steiner (1991, p.57) compared the nutritional effect of eating beetroot and potato. 'If one eats beetroot, one becomes filled with a desire to think ... If one eats potatoes, one only desires to eat again soon'. He said that beetroot has a fairly high salt content, which, on digestion, is transported quickly to the head, stimulating the brain. In contrast, the potato, being a tuber which is a swollen stem rather than a root, is digested more slowly in the abdomen. Some of the digestive process is carried over into the nervous system, dulling the ability to think. Steiner said that since society has been eating large quantities of potatoes our thinking has deteriorated and become more materialistic.

Cabbage

Cabbages are made up of leaves symmetrically arranged in the form of a huge bud. The leaves are quite solid; they have an earthy solidity. The leaves have a deep, slightly blue-green colour which indicates strong watery, fluid energies, which have combined with strong earthy energies. Cabbages have a slightly sulphurous smell and contain sulphur compounds. This indicates that warmth energies have been drawn down into the leaves. Some of these sulphur compounds have been identified as active phytochemicals called glucosinolates, which our bodies metabolise into powerful anti-carcinogens called isothiocyanates. Isothiocyanates increase the activity of the liver's Phase 2 detoxification enzymes, assisting the liver to detoxify harmful, cancer-causing compounds (IARC 1994, p.206). The fluid energies, which are strong in cabbages, stimulate chemical activity and could be expected to help the chemical activity of the liver.

Cabbages belong to the plant family Cruciferae. This family of plants is sturdy, relating to the forces of the earth without becoming subject to them and hardening into trees (Pelikan 1997, pp. 129, 132). They can take in powerful light forces and also show the swelling, actively growing forces of the watery element, which give them a rugged vitality. They show this vital energy in that their life rhythms are much faster than those of much other plants, for instance, their seeds germinate quickly. Crucifers have a sluggish protein process, making their proteins hard to digest, but the sulphur they contain helps the protein process.

The vegetables we use from the Cruciferae are interesting in that we use different parts of the plant. Cabbages are the leaves, brussels sprouts are axillary buds, cauliflower and broccoli the flower, and radishes are roots. One would expect them to share characteristics of the whole family, but to affect different parts of the body when eaten.

Lettuce

It is interesting to compare cabbages with the lettuce, *Lactuca sativa*. Lettuces generally have a more delicate, lighter green leaf. They are less solid to eat, without the sulphurous quality. Some lettuce varieties curl in on themselves to make a 'heart' in a similar way to cabbages, while the leaf varieties are all outward growing leaves. Some of the leaf varieties have red, indented leaves, looking as though they contain more light influence and less watery influence.

Lettuces are from a different plant family Asteracae (formerly Compositae) or daisy family. They have a quite different flower from that of the cabbage when it 'goes to seed'. The strong watery energies in lettuces make them refreshing and cooling to eat in summer. These days we tend to eat most fruit and vegetables all year round, but some people find that they feel more healthy when they eat 'seasonally'.

Lettuces are not often listed as being good sources of nutrients, but have strong watery or 'mercurial' energies. As Rudolf Steiner and Wilhelm Pelikan relate leafy vegetables to the rhythmic respiratory and blood circulatory processes in the human body, one could expect that the strong fluid energies in cabbage and lettuce would also assist those processes in the eater. These rhythmic processes hold the balance between our nerve, sense and thinking processes and our metabolic processes. It is hard to find scientific evidence to back up such assertions. This is partly because it would be difficult to isolate the effects of one component of the diet or to subject to a single plant in the diet and also because research concentrates on effects of particular chemical nutrients rather than the whole food.

Lettuces are good sources of vitamin K and folic acid (vitamin B9) which are needed for the metabolism of many chemical substances in our bodies. The watery energies are sometimes called chemical energies because they facilitate chemical transformations.

Peas

Peas are one of the most commonly eaten vegetables, as a bag of frozen peas in the freezer is so convenient. If you think about it for a moment you can see that peas are seeds, quite different from leafy and root vegetables, so could have a different nutritional effect. Kolisko (1978, p.46) said that seeds affect the urinary system because in the seed there is a changeover from building up complex proteins to breaking down again, as in the excretory system. For example, rosehips have traditionally been used as a remedy for kidney disease. Scientific research has recently confirmed this relationship: Canadian scientists have found that a pea protein extract fed to rats with severe kidney disease brought urinary function back to normal and reduced their related high blood pressure (Aukema & Aluko 2009).

If you look at pea flowers, they look rather like butterflies with a slightly animal like appearance (see Figure 8.2). The plant family they belong to has been renamed Papilonaceae (formerly Leguminoseae), reflecting their similarity to butterflies. Pea plants climb up into the air and light and produce lots of flowers and seed. The ends of the shoots are still bursting with growth energy and are growing more leaves while flowers are produced amongst the leaves lower down the stem. The strong growth and flowering energies are interacting more than in many other plants that only flower at the end of a stem when watery growth energies are exhausted. Pea plant roots can 'fix' nitrogen from the air. Bacteria in root nodules convert nitrogen gas to a form of nitrogen that can feed plants. This enables the pea plant to have a high protein content, which has to be digested differently from other vegetables: beans from the same family are well known for flatulence effects. Pelikan (1997, pp.320–24) discusses how these characteristics give pea plants animal-like energies. Their weak, climbing stems show a struggle between the forces of gravity and light.

When you eat peas you obtain more protein than from other vegetables: you also obtain air/light energies and the sensing, moving, energies generally found in animal food.

Figure 8.2: Drawing of a Pea flower.

Soya beans

Soya beans are widespread in our food. Most processed food includes soya beans in its list of ingredients and many people drink soy milk and eat soya products such as tofu as a substitute for animal protein. Soya beans are particularly rich in protein and the protein contains a good balance of all the essential amino acids. There is controversy over whether this advantage outweighs the disadvantages attributed to soya beans that include high levels of phytoestrogens, goitrogens which depress thyroid function and phytic acid which blocks absorption of calcium, magnesium, iron and zinc (Fallon & Enig 2000B).

I am wary of any product containing soya beans because the majority of the world supply, produced in North and South American countries, is now genetically modified. That apart, it is interesting to consider what Rudolf Steiner said about eating beans. He said that eating protein helps us to produce mental images and think, but if we eat too much protein, the mental images may become overwhelming (Steiner 1991, p.131). It is important that we are able to control our mental images and thinking.

Tomatoes

Tomatoes have become very popular and are eaten all year round. They contain high levels of nutrients, particularly lycopene, a carotenoid with strong antioxidant properties. Tomatoes are therefore considered to help to prevent cancers. But looking at the plant in the context of how it grows and its plant family gives a different picture. Tomatoes belong to the nightshade family (Solanaceae) which also includes potatoes. Many plants in this family such as deadly nightshade are highly poisonous. The poisons are alkaloids, which are nitrogenous breakdown products that seem to be produced as a result of processes that generally only occur in animals. Although tomatoes are not poisonous, they show some of the same rapid, exuberant growth characteristics of other members of the family.

101

Pelikan (1997, p.157) writes of the battle between the sprouting leaf growth and the overpowering flowering principle. Rudolf Steiner (1991, p.180) recommended that anyone with a tendency towards cancerous growths should avoid eating tomatoes because they stimulate independent growth, which is a feature of cancer. Tomato plants show this independent growth in that they grow best on raw manure and compost that has not been broken down.

Apples and oranges

Apples are one of my favourite foods. A really good apple seems very complete and refreshing, like a meal in itself. Apple trees belong to the Rosaceae family. The plants in this family seem particularly beautiful and harmonious. Pelikan (1997, p.227) wrote about their harmonious blend of earth, leaf, light and warmth energies. They have characteristic delicately scented 5-petalled flowers. If you cut around an apple's equator you see a beautiful, star-like form. This form is found in many plants that relate to the planet Venus, reflecting the pattern made by the movement of this planet around the earth (see Figure 8.3).

Scientists at the Louis Bolk Institute in Holland found that apples taste best when they have the optimum combination of sweetness and acidity (Bloksma *et al.* 2004, pp.55, 56). This happens when the earthly and watery growth energies are well integrated with the light and warmth energies that bring ripening and sweetness.

Contrast apples with oranges. They are both round and juicy, but quite distinct. No one would confuse one with the other. It is interesting to think what makes them different. The bright orange colour and less solid juiciness of an orange indicates that it contains more warmth energies than an apple. Orange trees need a warmer climate than apple trees to flourish. Their leaves are rounder with darker, thicker, shiny surfaces. They can survive a dryer, hotter climate than apple trees, whereas apples need a cooler climate to develop a good taste. The growing popularity of eating locally grown produce makes nutritional sense. Orange juice is particularly refreshing in a warm climate, whereas the more solid and storable apples are appropriate for a cooler climate.

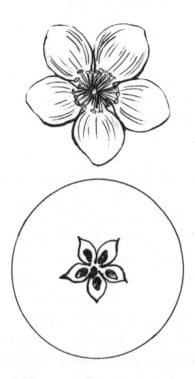

Figure 8.3: Drawing of an apple flower and cross-section through an apple.

Onions

Onions grow quite differently from the other plants discussed. They are members of the Liliacae family, which grow from bulbs. They are a very watery plant; Pelikan (1997, p.367) writes of their apparent desire to be a watery sphere. But they are not only watery, they have a strong sulphurous taste and smell. This sulphurous process gives them warmth. When eaten they work on the digestion and also on reducing mucous and congestion in the respiratory area. Hauschka (2002, p.87) discusses how the lily family of plants were traditionally regarded as plants of wisdom. Their strong aroma 'wakes up' the digestion and excretory systems and stimulates thinking.

Grains

In this chapter my main focus is on vegetables but I will briefly discuss the formative influences in grains, as they are an important part of many diets. Wheat, barley, oats and rye belong to the Graminaceae family, which also includes most of the pasture grasses that cattle and sheep eat. The long, spiky form of grass and grain leaves and the upright grain stalks indicate a strong light influence. Grain needs the warm, 'sulphur' energies to ripen.

Grains are an important source of plant protein. Wheat is symmetrical and compact around the upright stem, suggesting strong interaction of sunlight and warmth with salt forming earth energy whereas oats have a much looser form which suggests more interaction with watery and warmth energies. The grains contain high levels of starch. Hauschka (2002, p.88) pointed out that the formative patterns seen in their starch granules relate to those seen in the whole plant. Wheat has circular symmetrical starch grains, whereas oat starch granules have a radiating pattern, which indicates greater warmth energy influence. Oats also have a higher oil content and are more digestible than wheat, indicating more warmth energy in the grain (see Figure 8.4).

We generally think of potatoes, wheat, oats, rice and other grains as being almost interchangeable as sources of carbohydrates, but if you consider their energies, they are not. Grains are actually plant seeds so have different energies to potatoes, and the formative pattern in grain starch granules indicates that each grain could have a slightly different effect when eaten. Steiner commented that the carbohydrate in grains is in a form that people can transform into starch and sugar in a way that strengthens the head, in contrast to the weakening effect of eating potatoes (Steiner 1991, pp.101, 105). In grain plants the root energies work all the way up into the grains, so the grains are able to nourish our heads and thinking. It is therefore important that the grains used in our bread have been processed and baked in a way that does not destroy these energies.

The effects of different plant energies on nutrition would be an interesting, but difficult topic to research. It seems likely that other factors such as how much you enjoy a food, how well it is cooked and presented and how well it is digested could have just as much or more effect on nutritional outcome. However, you may be interested to observe whether you perceive any effects from eating different vegetable and food types.

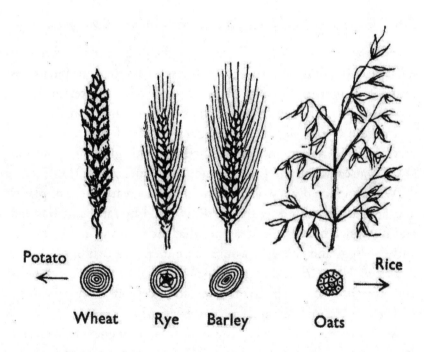

Figure 8.4: The nature of four types of grain and its expression in their starch kernels. From Nutrition *by Rudolf Hauschka (2002), Sophia Books, Forest Row, UK, p.88, Figure 9.*

9. Light Energy in Food

Have you noticed people who seem to glow with an inner vitality? Contrast this with the greyness of a sick person. A really good apple shines with vitality: this shine is different from the polished wax shine that is applied to apples to sell them. The radiance that is connected with life is like a reflection of the sunlight our world depends on.

Sunlight is essential for humans, animals and our food crops

Every morning, as a new day dawns, light picks out the forms of hills, trees, buildings and people. As the sun rises the light intensifies bringing a myriad of shades of different colours and textures. We recognise our friends and distinguish many plants and animals.

Imagine you are in a beautiful garden, full of fruit trees and a variety of vegetables, and surrounded by fields growing grass and grain. Pause a while and look around (see Figure 9.1).

What an incredible world we live in, with great variety of plants and animals, nurtured by the earth, watered by rain, and warmed and illumined by the sun. Imagine what the world would seem like without light and colour – would there even be any life? Certainly not as we know it now. Plants depend on light for photosynthesis and growth, and we depend on plants for our food. They provide us with grains, animal pasture, fruits and vegetables.

We are directly affected by the amount of light energy we receive from the sun. We all know that children need exposure to sunlight to make sufficient vitamin D for healthy bone development. Some Scandinavians become depressed in their long, dark winters. Most of us enjoy feeling the sun's warmth and seeing more cheerful faces

Figure 9.1: Sunlight on delicate pink apple petals, growing vegetables and swelling pumpkins.

when the sun shines after several days of cloudy weather. Light has been found to affect our pineal glands which control many hormones relating to our health and feelings.

We depend on sunlight to help build the plant foods we eat. Plants have developed as wonderfully efficient light processors, depending on light to build the carbohydrates, oils and protein they are composed of. In the process of photosynthesis, the green chlorophyll in plant leaves uses light energy to convert carbon dioxide and water to sugar and oxygen. Sunlight also activates energy cycles and enzyme activity in plants enabling them to build more complex substances such as proteins, oils and complex polysaccharide sugars from the simple sugars. These proteins, oils and sugars store and transmit light energy. We tend to take plants for granted, but we owe our life on earth to them. Not only do they provide oxygen for us to breathe, but food to nourish us and beautiful flowers and leaves to lift our spirits. Light appears to burst out of the bright yellow trumpet of a daffodil, nourishing our senses.

In the incredibly rich and diverse tastes and fragrance of freshly picked, ripe fruit we can experience the essence of the plant, woven from condensed sunlight.

Sunlight affects the way plants grow, drawing them upwards. Although plants can grow in artificial light, they are likely to differ from plants grown in sunlight, which contains a range of wavelengths, from far-red through to ultra-violet light. Plants are very sensitive to particular wavelengths and the variation in day length through the year. These provide signals for flowering and many other physiological activities. Full-spectrum lighting has been found to be necessary for human health. We need all the colours in sunlight, which may not be present in artificial lighting. Human health issues can sometimes be solved by exposure to a particular colour light.

Sunlight brings us ether and other energies as well as the light that we can see and measure. As discussed in Chapter 5, at the quantum level studied by quantum scientists, matter does not conform to most basic physical laws. When we only take into account what we can physically see and touch and measure, we may fail to understand the basis of living systems.

Farmers and agronomists focus mainly on soil fertility for growing crops – but light absorption is also crucial for growing plants. It is much harder to grow crops in the winter when there is less light and heat than in summer. The quantity and quality of light energy they receive affects the quantity and quality of light energy in the plant food we eat.

Light and shade effects

Many plants grow differently in shade compared to those growing in the full sun. Take the example of dandelions, illustrated in Chapter 5 (Figure 5.1). A dandelion growing in full sun has fairly small, flattish highly serrated leaves. Contrast these with leaves that have grown in the shade, that look a darker green, larger, more 'lush' and less serrated.

There are many other effects of light and shade. The following table shows the results of experiments that compared the effects of full daylight, half shade and deep shade, organic and mineral fertiliser on plant nutritional quality factors.

MORE LIGHT	LESS LIGHT
High dry matter content	Low dry matter content
Low crude protein content	High crude protein content
High true protein: crude protein	Low true protein: crude protein
Lower nitrate, amides, free amino acids content	Higher nitrate, amides, free amino acids content
Higher disaccharide sugars	Lower disaccharides
Lower monosaccharide sugars	Higher monosaccharides
High vitamin C content	High vitamin A content
Rich fragrance, taste	Poor fragrance, taste

Table 1. *Effects of light and shade factors on plant form and food quality (from Koepf 1993, p.38).*

Looking at the table above, can you form a picture in your mind of the different kinds of nutrition you would get from plants grown with more or less light? The main point is that light activates enzymes which enable complex proteins and sugars to be built up in plant food, providing better nutrition for animals and humans that eat the plant. If the soil is cool and moist and well fertilised, this also gives a 'shade' effect, and the plant needs more light to be able to process the nutrients it takes up from the soil than in dryer, warmer and less fertile conditions. Obviously very dry, hot conditions are not desirable: the soil fertility and moisture need to be sufficient to produce a crop.

Most commercial food growers aim to grow the maximum quantity of product in the shortest possible time, in order to make a profit. This is the result of many consumers looking to buy food as cheaply as possible. But in general, the more fertilisers and manures are used, and the quicker the crop is grown, the lower its quality. To grow a higher quality product, the plant needs time and plenty of light to develop complex sugars, proteins, oils and antioxidants. Would you rather buy cheap vegetables blown up with nitrogen and water or more expensive higher quality vegetables?

Light and protein quality, complex sugars and oils

The soil and food scientist Ehrenfried Pfeiffer, working in the USA in the 1950s, said that our plants, and the food we obtain from them, no longer contained sufficient light (Pfeiffer 1958, p.14). He said this is the basis of many human health problems. Have you ever thought about why we are building houses with bigger and bigger windows that let in more light, and why we now prefer brighter colours than our ancestors did? Maybe there is a connection with our health condition. Certainly there are large numbers of people needing anti-depressant pills: they could be lacking inner light.

Pfeiffer said that we need to ingest light energy to provide a stimulus for building our own protein. And this protein needs to contain the right balance of all the essential amino acids – the protein building blocks that we cannot make ourselves. Often our food does not contain this balance of amino acids. As protein is the basis of our immune systems, our genes and the functioning of every cell in our bodies this is a serious issue. Most of the research carried out by scientists such as Pfeiffer has been dismissed as it did not conform to the rigorous statistical design and analysis requirements that became commonly accepted in the latter part of the twentieth century. I believe that this often results in throwing the baby out with the bathwater, and that many older research results need to be validated by modern research.

Ehrenfried Pfeiffer spent many years researching and teaching about how our food plants need to contain strong 'light processes' to improve human nutrition. Pfeiffer (1958, p.16) found that applying biodynamic sprays to plants increased the content of the amino acids lysine, tryptophan and arginine, relative to the other amino acids in grains. Lysine and tryptophan are essential amino acids for human nutrition and arginine is essential for children. Pfeiffer was particularly concerned about how the content of lysine in grains had decreased. This is still recognised as a problem and maize corn has been genetically modified to contain more lysine for animal feed. The risks associated with genetic modification, producing protein that the body does not recognise and causing digestive problems, make it preferable to study how this problem of low lysine content has come about and how growing conditions can be changed to fix the problem. It is likely that a combination of plant breeding for other characteristics and using a lot of soluble nitrogenous fertilisers to grow grains have reduced the capacity of grain plants to build amino acids.

Light has an important role in the building up of many complex nutrients in a plant, in addition to protein. The fruit and seeds particularly, contain concentrated nutrients, including more complex sugars, proteins and oils than in leaves, which contain more simple sugars and starch. The light energy received by the plant affects how much of these complex nutrients develop. Many nutritional supplements now available contain 'phyto-nutrients' such as mannose, galactose, glycoproteins. These nutrients are in well-grown fruit and seeds which have been ripened by sunlight. Unfortunately fruit for transport and sale generally has to be picked before it is fully ripe so that it is not overripe before it is bought. This fruit generally contains less complex sugars and other nutrients than tree-ripened fruit. Much of our craving for sweet foods may be related to our need for these complex sugars, which is not satisfied by simple sugars.

Inner quality of food

In Chapter 3, I mentioned the research by Albert Popp and other quantum physicists who developed the delayed luminescence method. This measures the health of living cells through their pattern of emission of very small light photons. Using this method, free range eggs were found to have a significantly higher capacity to store light than eggs from battery caged chickens (Popp 1994, p.1290). Milk from pasture- fed cows shows a more coherent photon emission than milk from housed cows and potatoes treated with artificial fertilisers were found to emit more irregular biophotons than organically grown potatoes. Methods such as delayed luminescence may soon be used more widely to measure food quality and human health, as the importance of harmonious light energy in food becomes better understood.

Delayed luminescence was one of the measurement methods used by Dutch scientists to measure the 'inner quality' of apples grown in different ways (Bloksma *et al.* 2004). They defined inner quality as a high level of integration of growth and differentiation processes, that is, a continuous balanced relation between these two types of process. By 'differentiation' they meant ripening and formation of more complex compounds such as flavours and coloured pigments. In a similar study on carrots scientists found that carrots grown in more light showed a greater degree of differentiation and integration. Carrots grown in more light also had greater weight and length of root, sweetness, sugar content, carotene (and 'orangeness') content and dry matter, and better carrot taste and juiciness. Carrots grown at high light levels had less weight loss during storage. (Northcote *et al.* 2004, pp.46–58).

Differences in quality of animal food products such as milk may be due to the quantity and quality of light in the pasture and forage the cattle eat. In a British research study, the milk from cows kept on organic farms was found to contain a higher ratio of polyunsaturated fatty acids to monounsaturated fatty acids and a lower ratio of Omega-6 to Omega-3 fatty acids compared to milk from non-organic farms (Ellis *et al.* 2006). This indicates that there was more light energy in the pasture grown on the organic farms. On most modern dairy farms nitrogen fertiliser is applied to grow grass quickly and the cows graze the pasture when it is quite short, before it has absorbed much light to enable more complex nutrients to develop. Organic farmers do not apply nitrogen and are more likely to let the grass grow a bit longer before grazing. They may also feed their cows hay, which is made from longer grass that may contain grass seeds with high oil content.

Chickens kept in houses lit with full-spectrum lighting (containing all the colours of the spectrum) have been found to be calmer, live longer, lay more eggs and the eggs contain about 25% less cholesterol (Liberman 1991, p.59). The importance of this oil content of our diet has been stressed by Sally Fallon and Mary Enig, in their book, *Nourishing Traditions* (2000A) and through the Weston A. Price Institute.

Biodynamic farmers have developed an additional way to bring more light into food. This is discussed in the following chapter.

10. The Role of Silica in Bringing Light into Food

When plants are grown in sandy soils they generally look taller and thinner as though grown in plenty of light. They have long roots and they flower more easily compared to plants grown in clay soils. We do not generally see the roots of a growing plant. Their growth makes a big difference to how well the rest of the plant grows. The lettuce plants in the photo below show the longer roots of lettuces grown in a sandy soil compared to clay soil (see Figure 10.1).

Figure 10.1: Lettuce plants grown in clay soil, sandy soil and sand with compost.

Silica, or silicon, is the main constituent of sand. Silica forms beautiful hexagonal crystals – such as quartz and amethyst. Quartz crystals have been used since very early times to amplify, clarify and store energy. The silica in sand stores the sun's light and warmth, which are needed for plant growth, particularly for roots. Root crops like carrots and potatoes grow better in sandy soil.

Silica used to be considered inert and not important for plant, animal and human health. More recently, scientists are recognising that silica is an essential nutrient. A lack of it in our food could be contributing to the adverse health effects of insufficient light in our food.

Silica in human health

Silica (silicon) is particularly important for the metabolism of human and animal bones and for stimulating collagen synthesis (Reffitt *et al.* 2003). Collagen is the main component of cartilage, ligaments, tendons, bone and skin. Collagen is important for skin strength and elasticity, and its degradation leads to wrinkles that accompany aging. Silica helps to prevent osteoporosis. It is unfortunate that so many people have only focused on taking calcium to protect against osteoporosis as several other factors are involved, including an adequate supply of silica. Silica strengthens blood vessel walls. It enables the sheen of healthy hair, prevents brittle nails, and strengthens tooth enamel (Kaufmann 1993). Silica deficiency can be a factor in poor immune systems, poor digestion and urinary infections.

Silica is best absorbed by the body in plant form, so silica rich plants such as horsetail *(Equisetum arvense)* are helpful taken as a tea (see Figure 10.2). I was surprised to notice that my skin felt much softer after I drank horsetail tea for the first time. To have such a noticeable effect, my diet must have been deficient in silica.

Figure 10.2: Drawing of Horsetail (Equisetum arvense).

Silica in plant health

The important roles silica plays in plants have only been discovered recently. There are now many scientists studying its use as a fertiliser, and silicate fertilisers are being used particularly for growing sugar cane in Australia and rice in China. Applying large quantities of nitrogen, phosphorus and potassium to grow crops only works for a while, until the soil runs short of other minerals such as silica, boron, calcium, and magnesium that are needed, generally in small amounts.

Silica provides the strengthening for plant stems. Modern wheat plant varieties have been bred with shorter stalks because soils have become depleted of silica and stems are weaker than previously, tending to fall down before harvest. Silica protects plants from susceptibility to pests and disease both by strengthening plant cell walls and by assisting the production of phenolic compounds which have antioxidant and protective effects. Silica also assists plants to use the energy from elements such as phosphorus and nitrogen to build amino acids and proteins (Watanabe *et al.* 2001).

A lot of information is involved in building every protein

molecule in living organisms. We are using silicon chips to store incredible amounts of information in our computers in a structured way. I don't think we fully appreciate the role of silica in storing and transmitting energy and information in our earth and plants and in our own bodies.

As silica is an inert mineral it generally has to be activated in some way to be effective. Japanese and Russian scientists have found ways to activate silicon. In Europe a small group of farmers developed a technique for activating silica to enhance crops in the 1920s, as part of biodynamic farming.

Biodynamic farming and silica

Biodynamic farmers spray crops with a very dilute solution of specially prepared silica called the biodynamic preparation 501. This is made by grinding quartz crystals to a fine powder, making it into a slurry with water which is inserted into a cow horn. The cow horn is then buried in fertile, organically managed soil for about six months during summer. After removal from the horn the preparation is stirred rhythmically in water and applied in early morning as a fine spray in the air over the plants to be treated. This is done to enhance the quality attributes from 'light' effects. Research has shown that this silica treatment has similar effects on plants to the light effects described in the previous chapter.

Rudolf Steiner's recommendations for biodynamic farming (Steiner 1993) include enhancing and balancing the energies flowing up from the earth and down from the sun and stars, using special preparations, so that the soil becomes more 'enlivened' and 'dynamic' and plants are sensitised to take up nutrients from the soil and the air. The first preparation that farmers generally apply is preparation 500, which enhances soil and 'calcium' activity. This is made by filling a cow horn with cow-dung from an organically managed cow and burying it in the soil during the winter months. The preparation is then stirred rhythmically in water and sprayed on to soil or pasture. The preparation needs to be applied before the 501 silica preparation is used, to stimulate the earth growth energies flowing up into the plant. These energies are then counterbalanced by the light, shaping energies of the preparation 501.

Properties of silica

Try to visualise silica, not just as a solid crystal or particles as sand, but as a particular energy, that gives rise to particular effects that we can see or experience in some way. Silica has a range of effects on our earth, on plants and on humans. Most other minerals similarly have many effects. They are all symptoms or end results of the mineral processes.

Silica forms crystals and living structures

The formation of translucent hexagonal quartz crystals is a silica process that is happening all the time as a result of energies from the stars raying into our earth. Rudolf Steiner taught the view held by alchemists from early times, that minerals are the end-result of energy processes coming from the stars and planets. For example, iron deposits in the earth are the result of energies rayed to earth by the movement of the planet Mars.

Some people have difficulty in understanding and accepting these unseen energies or 'forces' as real, but the farmers and scientists who have worked with the biodynamic preparations have observed positive results. The very small quantities of preparations used work on these mineral processes. Now that scientists understand and work with electromagnetic forces for many purposes it is easier to comprehend that the planets continually rotating around us are sending our world continually changing patterns of energies, generated by planet movements and their interaction with energies from the stars. These energy patterns generate the mineral processes in the soil and plants that enable plant growth.

In his book *Nature of Substances in Agriculture* (2002), Rudolf Hauschka recounted how he spent many years repeating over and over again the mineral analysis of plant ash (pp.15–20). He found considerable variation in levels of various minerals in this ash at different times when measured from the same plants under the same conditions. He then carried out experiments in which he germinated seeds in dishes of distilled water covered by glass bowls. The quantities of calcium, magnesium and phosphorus in the seeds changed as the seeds germinated. In further experiments he weighed growing plants in enclosed jars using a very sensitive balance and found their weights varied. He made regular measurements over seven years and found that the weight variations corresponded with day and night and with seasonal, moon and planet rhythms. He concluded that as physical matter can appear and disappear according to these rhythms, there must be an unseen aspect of the plant that carries the plant energy. This energy appears as physical matter then withdraws again in regular rhythms. He carried out these trials over seven years and observed that each year results were slightly different. He attributed these differences to differences in planetary positions.

These experiments indicate that there is an energy process of a substance that precedes the physical deposit of the substance. The quantity of a substance in a plant or animal may not reflect the effect that substance has on the organism. An energy process that has a large effect on plants and animals, such as silica, may only be present in very small quantities. The effects of the silica process can be seen in living organisms, for example bees, which build a hexagonal cell structure in their honeycombs. Rudolf Steiner (1993, pp.21, 22) also pointed out that the presence of silica in the earth enables plant stems to grow straight upwards and develop full seed-heads and grains. The silica process forms the beautiful structure of plants and animals. The structures generally contain very little silica but have been shaped by silica energies. These energies flow from the stars and from the presence of silica in the earth.

Silica stores and transmits light

You may have experienced a feeling of more light and energy when standing on rocks containing a lot of silica. I have certainly felt this energy. Nicolaus Remer (1995, pp.37, 38) wrote about how silica transmits light and heat in soils. It is easy to verify this by walking barefoot without sunglasses on a beach in the summer sun! The presence of silica in the earth brings and stores light and warmth energies from the sun and outer planets (Mars, Jupiter and Saturn) into the earth (Steiner 1993, p.22).

Eugen and Lili Kolisko (1978, pp.71–79) in their *Agriculture of Tomorrow,* relate many investigative experiments they carried out to seek understanding of how the light transmission capacity of silica affects growing plants. They grew wheat seedlings in dishes containing soil in which finely ground sand had been mixed and placed in varying degrees of light and darkness. They compared the seedling growth with that of seedlings grown in exactly the same conditions, except no sand had been added to the soil. The seedlings grown without sand and without much light had longer internodes (the stem between the nodes where new leaves develop), the second leaf was shorter than the first leaf and root development was poor in comparison with seedlings grown in more light. In contrast, the seedlings grown in dishes that included sand did not show such extreme characteristics when grown in the dark – they appeared as though they had been grown in more light, with more root growth, shorter internodes and longer second leaves. This research was done before the modern methods of statistical design were developed. I have seen this effect myself in a small preliminary trial: it would be interesting to repeat it in a statistically designed trial.

Silica scatters and polarises light

Silica aerogels are used in industry because of their 'Rayleigh scattering' effects, which causes the reddening of transmitted light (Hunt and Ayers, 2003). This scattering effect, and the well-known light polarising effect of quartz crystals, may explain some of the effects of spraying the biodynamic silica spray in the air above plants.

Silica stores and transmits information

We know that tiny silicon chips store and transmit large quantities of information in computers. A further property of silica described by Hauschka (2002, pp.121–26) is seen when it has been crushed very finely and mixed with water to form a colloidal solution. It tends to spread out over surfaces, forming thin skins, as it has high surface tension. Through this effect of colloidal silica, very small amounts of silica deposits in plant cell walls can have a considerable effect on the functioning of the cells. Bruce Lipton in his *Biology of Belief* (2005, p.91) relates the discovery that the cell membrane is a structural and functional homologue of a silicon chip: that both are crystal semiconductors with gates and channels that regulate the substances passing in and out of the cell. They are sensitive to environmental signals, which can have a greater effect on cell functioning than the DNA in genes.

This sensitivity of cell membranes could extend to receiving energy signals from planets and stars. Rudolf Steiner talked about the importance of planetary energies, assisted by the silica spray, for building nutritious food plants. He said, for example, that the taste developed in different fruits has been influenced by the planets they relate to: apple taste is a Jupiter quality, plum taste has a Saturn quality (Steiner 1993, p.40). Mars energies stimulate plant protein formation, Jupiter influences taste and essential oils.

These properties of silica relate more to the silica energy process than to the deposited substance. It is often more effective to work with energy processes rather than the substances. Steiner (1993, pp.91–93) indicated that it is more effective for farmers to stimulate the enlivening energy processes than to apply mineral fertilisers. The energy processes increase the mineral processes and the activity of the soil bacteria, fungi and other soil organisms, which make nutrients available to plants.

Effects of the biodynamic silica spray on plants

When farmers spray the biodynamic silica preparation 501 on to plants, they make a fine spray up in the air over the plants, at sunrise. I have spent several years trying to understand how the silica preparation works and what it actually does to plants. There has been insufficient research to explain exactly how silica affects plant physiology. Like all living processes, it tends to have different effects under different conditions and it is difficult to separate out its effects from those of many other factors.

I suspect that as well as there being a direct effect of the activated silica energy on the plant, the spray changes the effect of the sunlight on the plant in some way. Several researchers have found that the spray does not seem to affect the photosynthesis rate in a plant. However, it seems that it may slightly change the wavelengths of light reaching a plant. I have measured the levels of different wavelengths in the visible light spectrum reflected by lettuce plant leaves before and after spraying some plants with the silica preparation, and some with water. This gives an indication of how much of each wavelength is absorbed by the leaves. I was unable to spend long enough on this activity to obtain scientifically acceptable results, but it appeared there could have been changes in wavelength levels at both the far red and ultraviolet ends of the spectrum in plants sprayed with the biodynamic silica.

When the silica solution is sprayed above plants it would have a scattering effect on sunlight in a similar way to the aerogels used in industry. This results in small changes to the light properties, such as an increase in light wavelengths at the red end of the spectrum. This can trigger plant responses. Small changes in light wavelength have been shown to affect plant hormone and enzyme activity, respiration and DNA transcription (Lillo & Appenroth 2001). Of particular importance is a stimulation of the enzyme, nitrate reductase, in plant leaves that changes nitrates to ammonia as the first step towards forming amino acids and proteins. This could explain why some researchers have found that spraying the 501 preparation enhances organic acid, amino acid and protein formation A trial comparing beans grown using all the biodynamic preparations with beans grown hydroponically, found more methionine and cysteine in the biodynamically grown beans. These sulphur containing amino acids are particularly important in the diet (Stolz *et al.*).

Scientific studies have found that the silica spray affects the water uptake of plants through its effect on plant leaf stomata (Koenig 1988). Very small changes in light wavelengths have been found to trigger cell signals that affect the opening of plant stomata. Stomata are very small holes in plant leaves that take in carbon dioxide for photosynthesis and release water into the air. After I sprayed some lettuce plants with the horn silica twice during a dry spring, there was an observable difference in their form. The sprayed plants became compacted with smaller, harder leaves compared to plants not sprayed. This was an extreme effect of too much spray, which growers would not want to use on their crops!

The horn silica spray enables the harmonious ordering of plant energy, assisting the building of harmonious plant protein. It appears that very small amounts of silica deposits in plant cell walls have a considerable effect on the functioning of the cells. The functioning of silica in cell membranes described by Bruce Lipton could explain why spraying plants with silica results in better functioning of plant cells to produce more nutrients. It could also explain why plants sprayed with silica are more sensitive to the energies coming from the sun and planets that enable building of high quality plant products.

Past research has shown that the horn silica spray improved flowering, ripening and flavour of fruit, vegetable and grain crops, but only when good compost or manure and the horn manure preparation were previously applied and when there was sufficient moisture (Pettersson 1978).

Nicolas Remer researched the effects of the silica spray for many years, finding it enhanced organic acid and protein formation (Remer 1995, p.55). Some of Remer's research used homeopathic dilutions of the silica preparation. He found a D7 solution the most effective. This is one gram of silica dissolved in 1000 litres of water. It is prepared by a series of steps, each time mixing 1 part to 10 and shaking rhythmically. I have struggled for some time to understand how homeopathy can work, and many scientists do not accept it, but I have seen its effects on plant growth and on human and animal health. More and more people now use homeopathic remedies themselves, and farmers use them effectively for their livestock. Remer found that in general, the less matter in a solution the more energy it has.

Remer undertook many trials using the homeopathic silica and showed that it assisted the building up of organic acids, iron, amino acids and protein in plants (pp.56–67). Increases of amino acid levels of 30–100% were measured after applying the homoeopathic solution to Savoy cabbages.

Remer also discussed how there has been a considerable decline in silica content of European soils that have been cultivated for a long time. This has had adverse effects on grass and grain quality and stalk rigidity and on animal health. This leads me to think that an important benefit of using the preparation 501 is that it increases the silica energies working in the soil and around plants on a whole farm or garden, in addition to its effects on the particular plants sprayed. When farmers and gardeners work to enliven their soils and bring all the various energies into balance and harmony, this will affect the quality of all their crops and animals.

Light and Vitamin C

In Chapter 8 I discussed the connection between vitamin C and light energy. It is interesting that both vitamin C and silica have been found to assist synthesis of the major protein, collagen, in animals (Barnes pp.264–67). We keep finding when studying organisms that many different chemical elements and compounds work together in living processes. Possibly silica and vitamin C enable more effective light transmission, which brings information and energy to enable the building of protein.

In view of the discoveries of the role of silica in plants, it seems likely that milk and other products produced on biodynamic farms where the silica preparation is used would contain high quality Omega oils and proteins. The connection between light and vitamin C formation could mean that products from such farms would also contain higher levels of vitamin C and antioxidant activity. Scientific investigation of such possibilities could yield exciting results.

More research needed

More scientific research is also needed for better understanding of how silica affects plants and food quality. At present I find the best explanation is that silica spray improves the quantity and quality of light absorbed by plants. This activates differentiation processes that results in increased protein, complex sugar and oil production. The preparation 501 spray also makes plants more sensitive to formative and mineral process energies from the planets so they grow better roots which take up more nutrients from the soil and can produce well-integrated, harmonious and nutritious food.

11. Nutrition for Wholistic Health and Future Generations

The way food is grown does make a difference

Let's return again to the questions raised in Chapter 1 about why people find they feel healthier eating food grown by biological, organic and biodynamic methods, in spite of there being little evidence of differences from standard food nutrient measurements. If we rely on these nutrient tests we fail to recognise that living plants, animals and humans are maintained by energies that are not directly measurable. Life and food production depend on 'formative forces' or 'organisational energies' coming from the stars and planets above us and the earth beneath our feet. Health is maintained when organisms are sensitive to and have a strong connection with these energies and when the energies are in balance. The main purpose of nutrition is to stimulate and regulate our own organisational energies.

Farming methods that stimulate and strengthen the plant formative forces will provide us with better nutrition than farming with a lot of chemical fertilisers and pesticides, which tend to reduce the sensitivity of plants to energies from the stars and planets. When plants are grown in healthy soil that is alive with soil life and contains a good mineral balance, their roots form an intimate connection with the soil and are exposed to strong earth growth energies. Treating plants and soil with biodynamic preparations increases their sensitivity to formative forces and mineral processes. A good balance can be achieved between the energies coming up from the soil and those coming in from the stars and planets. The silica spray regulates the light process, enabling building of coherently ordered protein containing essential amino acids and of oils.

In the research into inner quality of apples and carrots discussed in Chapter 3, the scientists concluded that high inner quality of carrots on clayish soils can be obtained with limited nutrients (no additional fertiliser or manure), possibly fewer plants per hectare, and late harvest. This might result in a lower yield. The evidence highlights an important issue for nutrition. High quality food takes longer to grow and may have a smaller volume than much of the food at present bought and consumed. Food quality has been sacrificed to enable us to buy cheap food. If we want higher quality we should pay more for it. But in terms of the nutritional benefits from high quality food, it may be no more expensive than food of lesser quality.

Organisational energy and quantum coherence

In Chapter 5, I discussed how quantum scientists have found that matter behaves in an organised, wholistic way, at a very small, quantum level. It seems likely that such behaviour relates to organisational energies. Several scientists have described concepts of such organising energies, such as 'morphic fields' (Sheldrake 2009), 'Subtle Organising Energy Fields' (Cousens 2000), and 'ethers' (Marti 1984).

Every year more scientific evidence appears supporting the theory of the quantum interconnectedness of the universe. Interconnectedness may be due to the energies streaming in to the earth from far away in the universe. It may be connected to the movements of stars and planets in our universe, to the 'Music of the Spheres' that Kepler described.

The way that these organisational energies enable inner structuring and integration of plants and animals may be better understood when the findings of quantum physics are applied to living organisms.

Quantum theory states that the energy of absorbed light exists in two places at once – a quantum superposition state, or coherence – and such a state lies at the heart of quantum mechanical theory (Bohm 1980). Two waves are said to be coherent if they have a constant relative phase. The degree of coherence is measured by how perfectly the waves can cancel each other due to destructive interference. Scientists are now finding that quantum physics does apply to plant activities such as photosynthesis. They have found that energy patterns in distant molecules fluctuate in ways that show a connection to each other, something only possible through quantum coherence (Engel *et al*, 2007). This coherence occurs during photosynthesis.

Research by Albert Popp using delayed luminescence measurements, discussed in Chapter 3, has measured coherence of biophoton emissions in plants, animals and humans. The Popp research group has recorded biophoton measurements from human bodies, healthy and cancerous cells, animals, plants and food products He found that the biophoton field reflects all the biological rhythms in a living body. He said an essential basis of life is the 'active' capacity of the living system for constructive and destructive interference of biophotons (Popp & Chiang 1998, p.249).

Marco Bischof in his book *Biophotons: The Light in our Cells* (1995), explains how biophoton light is stored in the DNA molecules of cells, constantly releasing and absorbing a dynamic web of light. This web of light serves as the organism's main communication network and as the principal regulating instance for all life processes. He talks of a coherent holographic biophoton field of the brain and the nervous system, which may be the basis of memory and other phenomena of consciousness.

Our biophoton fields and biological rhythms and how they are affected by the food we eat needs a lot more investigation. Imagine the chaos introduced into these rhythms by eating artificial food additives or genetically engineered food, with structures that our body does not recognise.

Coherent light energy in food and our health

If food is grown for the right length of time by biological, organic and biodynamic systems that foster living energy processes, it is likely to contain more integrated, coherent light energy than food grown with chemical fertilisers. Each plant and its constituent cells have a particular organisational energy. Have you noticed how some plants grow better and resist pests better than others, even when they are all treated the same? Maybe these plants have a more coherent energy than other plants. Biologists have found that the organisation of a cell's structure affects how the cell responds to stimuli and how it expresses characteristics carried by its genes. (Lloyd *et al*, 2001).

The effect of light intensity and wavelength on formation of high quality protein, antioxidant compounds, essential oils and complex sugars, discussed in the previous chapters, makes it important that our food is grown with sufficient light energies.

The unseen integrating energies in light can be experienced through the effects of colour healing. Charles Klotsche (1992 pp.38–44) has related different colour frequencies to musical tones. He described how each colour and musical note emit vibrations that affect the functioning of our bodies and feeling state. When they are harmonious, or 'coherent' we feel well. The regular patterns made by tones, seen in Alexander Lauterwasser's sound water pictures (2006) appear to show a coherent state. Ernst Marti, the scientist who studied ether energies, said that: 'Music exists only by virtue of intervals, distances, simultaneity and sequence. Music is based on a force that separates ... while the separate parts retain their relationship' (Marti 1984, p.19). If we view our own bodies as being based on similar energy vibrations, we can see how the relationships and rhythms of such vibrations, their coherence, makes a big difference to our health.

This coherence is particularly important for our immune systems. Many diseases result from poorly functioning immune systems, and it seems likely that they are affected by the food we eat. If a protein in food does not have exactly the right dynamic structure the body is unable to digest it properly and the body's immune system does not recognise it and attacks it. Eating food containing chaotic energies may upset the coherent rhythms of our energy fields sufficiently to contribute to cancer and auto-immune diseases.

Nutrition, thinking and mental states

The effect of food on any particular person is an interaction between the energies in that food and the mental, emotional and physical health state of that individual. This is why there is such variability of effects and we can only predict average outcomes, but no-one is an average person.

Our beliefs and thinking, our fears and anxieties, our stresses and emotions all affect the conditions in our intestines, how we assimilate nutrients and how they are used in our bodies. The food we choose to eat interacts with all those aspects of ourselves. George Watson found that mental states such as schizophrenia can be altered by a change of diet (Watson, 1972). He also discovered that these interactions are complex, as the same diet has different effects on different people with the same condition. Watson's book *Nutrition and Your Mind* discusses his experiences with diet related mental conditions. He found that providing particular vitamins or other nutrients changed the condition, and that the nutrients needed for a particular condition varied between different individuals.

We all experience times when we can think clearly and other times when the mind is 'fuzzy' or we are too emotionally charged to think straight. Sometimes I can relate such states to what I have been eating. Emotions and thinking can affect our digestions, but also our diet affects emotions and thinking.

Rudolf Steiner described how potatoes and beetroot affect our thinking differently through the way that they are digested (Steiner 1991, pp.56, 57). The energy from digesting beetroot goes to the head and stimulates thinking (discussed in his Chapter 7, p.4). Because the potato is not a real root it has different energies which do not flow to the head, so does not stimulate thinking. The best way to test such an assertion is to observe the effects of eating particular vegetables on yourself. I have certainly noticed that after eating potatoes I feel particularly satisfied and comfortable but not stimulated to think. However, as everyone's digestion is different, such effects may be more marked in some people than others.

Stimulation of our inner light

The connection between how much light there is in our food and our mental and emotional states was also discussed by Rudolf Steiner. He said that when the sunlight energy is released during digestion of food, it stimulates our inner light (Steiner 1991, pp.143–45). What did he mean by 'inner light'? A plant's whole system is built up and run by sunlight, which stimulates it from outside. Steiner called the energy system that maintains a plant its 'etheric body' (see his Chapter 5, p.8). Animals and humans, in contrast, have inner regulated systems, run by our internal organs and nervous system. According to Steiner, humans and animals have etheric bodies like plants. He spoke of the human etheric body, or body of formative forces, as a 'delicate body of light' (Steiner 1980). Humans also have 'astral bodies' which provide this inner regulation and also sensing, movement and consciousness. The inner light is the energy that maintains this system. Steiner said that this inner light is an opposite force to the external sunlight. When we eat a plant, the plant energies that were built from sunlight into carbohydrates, fats and protein are digested and broken down before they are used to build up our own bodies. The inner light, or astral body, carries out this breaking down process, which stimulates our nervous system, our consciousness and thinking. Eating fresh plants with strong organisational, light energies requires the astral body to work harder to break it down, thus stimulating a healthy nervous system with the ability to be conscious and think clearly.

According to Rudolf Hauschka, vitamin C activity is linked with this activity of stimulating inner light (Hauschka 1998, p.127).

When someone's skin is exposed to strong sunlight it turns brown. Similarly, when people have scurvy their skin looks a yellow brown and starts to break down and bleed. When the skin has a healthy pink glow there is sufficient inner light to counteract the effects of outer light.

Stimulation of our consciousness and thinking through stimulation of our inner light is an important reason to eat and digest food containing strong organisational energies. Steiner recommended treating the soil, compost and plants we use to grow food with biodynamic preparations that increase their 'aliveness' and connection with the energies of the sun, planets and stars. Using these preparations enhances the stimulating effect of the food on our consciousness and thinking. I believe there is huge potential to improve the quality of our food using organic growing systems that include use of activated silica to bring more light energy into food plants. It is ironic that our society has become so clever in using the silicon chip in our computers to think and calculate for us, but silica's role in growing food that enables people themselves to think and become more conscious is not yet recognised.

Feeding the soul and spirit

If we recognise that we are more than our physical bodies, then we also need to consider nourishment of our souls and spirits. Our thoughts and environment are important for this nourishment, but our food also has an important effect on soul and spiritual health.

Whether you develop an understanding of quantum physics and the energy basis of life or whether you recognise a spiritual basis of people and the world around us, many people now recognise there is more to life than just the physical matter we see and touch and measure. This physical matter is like the visible tip of the iceberg. I am convinced that each one of us, and our whole universe, has a spiritual foundation, that life is generated and maintained by harmonious energy flows that have a spiritual basis. When these energies diminish or are altered to become disharmonious we and the world around us become sick, vulnerable to disease and decay.

The word 'spirit' means different things to different people. Steiner recognised a spiritual element in all the life around us, quoting Goethe's saying: 'matter cannot exist and operate without spirit, nor spirit without matter' (Steiner 1982). I have deliberately avoided using this term because of its varying connotations for different people. But I think it is important to try to keep separate in one's mind the energies that he referred to that are not physically measurable at all, from what are measurable effects such as photon emissions, that may be stimulated by the spiritual energies.

All our main world religions explain this spiritual basis of life well but differently. That is why they have survived and provided people with satisfactory meaning for existence. Our world did not happen by some cosmic accident. We are all connected to an overall design and organisation, a unifying spiritual basis of life. Our nutrition should help to connect us to this spiritual foundation of our world. Each person has a small speck of the universal spirit as the hidden basis of their being.

Many traditional religions preach an attitude of reverence to the life that has created our food. The practice of saying grace before a meal brings this attitude of reverence. What a difference it makes for a family to sit around a meal table, bless the food and eat together, rather than everyone snatching food from the fridge when hungry or eating in front of the TV! It not only helps to keep the family communicating together, it generally helps digestion and satisfaction from the meal. Do you notice what you are eating, the different flavours and textures of different foods? That can also help digestion and consciousness. The more I am conscious of what I am eating the more I enjoy it and feel a reverence for the plants and animals that have produced it.

Blessing the food can have more of an effect than we generally realise. Water crystallisation pictures by Andreas Schulz (2003, p.154) have shown clear improvement in the structure of water after it was blessed. (See Chapter 14 below.)

All the major religious traditions have had rules about what food should be eaten. These have generally stipulated particular foods that should be avoided. When those religions were founded, plants and animals were generally grown in natural environments, in contrast to the factory farming prevalent now. So now it is not only important that you eat the right foods, but also that they were grown and cooked in ways that ensure they contain the nutritive energies that they should.

When a person is healthy and well-nourished they sparkle with an inner light. We remark that they look well. This light enables them to think clearly, to be a fully conscious, responsible person and to relate well to other people and to their own soul and spirit. Stimulation by strong energy flows of well-grown, light-filled food is needed to develop your soul and spirit. Our bodies are maintained by streams of life energies flowing around them. To maintain the physical body our nutrition needs to cater for these life energies. Our consciousness is maintained by light energies that originated in the stars and planets of the universe. Our spiritual selves are nourished through reverence for the living plants and animals around us and through eating food grown with love and care and filled with spiritual warmth and light. What appears to us as light is the outer expression of a spiritual energy which affects the human spirit, enabling us to build our inner integrity: who we are as an individual.

This concept of a human individual self, which has memory and becomes aware of itself as an individual person was termed our 'ego body' by Steiner (1972, pp.28–35). Rudolf Steiner said that the spiritual development of the ego is stimulated through digestion of plant food (Steiner 1991, pp.144–50). He discussed how a vegetarian diet assists this process, that the effort involved in breaking down plant food to produce inner light and warmth and to build their own fat from this food, enables a mastery of one's own body and clearer, more flexible thinking. Eating animal protein requires less effort to break it down because it is more similar to our own protein and if we eat animal fat, we don't have to build our own fat. It enables more assertiveness and physical activity but does not stimulate thinking. However he stressed that we are all different and a vegetarian diet does not suit everyone.

Cosmic nutrition

A further aspect of Steiner's teaching about nutrition was that much of our bodies are built not from physical substance but from 'cosmic substance' from the universe around, that we take in through our breath and senses. He said the food we eat just provides stimulation for our bodies and substance we need for maintaining the structure and function of our heads and nervous system. The carbohydrates, protein, fats, oils and minerals we eat are needed, not to provide the physical substance of our bodies but to provide the energy and stimulation to enable us to build our bodies from the etheric energies and light around us (Steiner 1991, pp.58, 59).

This is something I have struggled to believe could be true. But when I try to understand the human body, and all matter, as energy, I can see that our solidity is a delusion. Physicists have found that atoms are mainly empty space (Lipton p.101). Richard Gerber (2001, pp.58, 59) talks of matter as 'frozen light', a term similar to Steiner's who said the heart is compressed light (Steiner 1991, p.59). The energy processes of all the minerals we need in our bodies are continually streaming into our earth and we can take in what we need and condense it to form the material of our bodies.

Such a concept underlines for me how little we yet grasp of how we are, how we are related to the world and universe around us, the interconnectedness of our thoughts, our feelings, our surroundings and our nutrition. The light that streams on to our earth, lighting up our surroundings with such a wonderful diversity of colours provides the spiritual foundation of our nutrition. When we stimulate our bodies with good nutrition they are alive with coherent energy. This is not only important for our own health, but for what we pass on to our children.

Inter-generational effects

It appears that the effects of our poor nutrition is showing up in the increasing number of small children with serious health issues. It is likely not an issue of what food they have eaten, nor the bugs they are exposed to, but the nutrition of their parents, and grandparents. Various feeding experiments with small animals that span several generations have shown the dramatic decline in health, vitality and fertility in second, third and fourth generations following poor diet of the original animals. A classic example is Francis Pottenger's cat experiment (Pottenger 1983). He found that cats fed cooked meat developed various health problems, whereas another group of cats fed raw meat kept healthy. He bred from these two groups of cats. By the third generation, the cats fed cooked meat were developing degenerative diseases very early in life, some were born blind and weak and had a much shorter life span. Many of them were unable to produce offspring. Since that experiment was done it has been discovered that a deficiency of the amino acid, taurine in cats' food causes similar problems, so it may have been lack of taurine rather than cooking the meat that was the problem. Whatever the reason, it does show an inter-generational effect of poor diet.

Scientists have shown that environmental influences, including nutrition, can modify genes. These modifications can be passed on to the next generation. For example, they compared the records of men who had died from diabetes and cardiovascular disease with a group of men who remained healthy. They found that the men who died generally had grandparents who had a plentiful supply of food when they were boys. The grandparents of the healthier men had a restricted diet as boys (Pembrey 2002). The diet of the grandparents who had plentiful food appears to have been too plentiful and to have adversely affected the genetic disposition to disease of their grandsons.

A further inter-generational effect discovered is gene imprinting in mammals. It is thought to influence the transfer of nutrients to the foetus and the newborn from the mother. Imprinted genes can affect growth in the womb and behaviour after birth. Aberrant imprinting disturbs development and has been found to be the cause of various disease syndromes (Wolf & Walter 2001).

It is one thing to suffer the consequences of one's own poor diet but a much bigger issue to think that many of us have laid the foundations for lives of poor health and misery for our grandchildren. To pass on the basis for health to your children and grandchildren you need to consider your own health, energies and diet.

PART 3.

BUYING, GROWING AND COOKING
YOUR OWN FOOD

12. How do you Choose Food?
Source, Taste and Aroma

You're standing in the middle of a street market or, more likely, a supermarket, surrounded by fruit and vegetables. There are various red or green leaf lettuces and cheaper hearted lettuces. How do you decide which to buy: or which apples?

Think about what really influences you. Do you look for quality and how do you assess it? An important question is whether the standard ways of measuring food nutrient contents are helpful, relevant and accessible to the buyer.

I once tested lettuce leaves from different sources for vitamin C content. To my surprise I found that the heart leaves from a fairly tired looking cheap lettuce from the supermarket contained more vitamin C than leaves from a nicer looking lettuce for almost twice the price from an organic shop. Maybe the organic lettuces were less fresh than the supermarket lettuces; maybe they were a variety with less vitamin C or maybe they were grown in poorer soil. There are many factors that affect food quality and visual appearance can be deceptive. Unfortunately you cannot always be certain that an organic product is better.

The best way to ensure a good food supply is to grow it yourself or to find a local producer who cares about their soil, plants and animals and producing high quality food. Seeing plants and animals growing before they are harvested and eaten gives you a good idea of their quality. I recently enjoyed some meat that was very different from any meat I had tasted before and so tender that my knife just slid through it instead of being pushed. This meat has been found to have a lower Omega-6: Omega-3 fatty acid ratio than fish, and much lower than most other grass-fed beef. Eating food with a high Omega-6: Omega-3 ratio increases your risk of heart disease, cancer and autoimmune disease (Simopoulos 2006). I visited the farm on which this beef was produced and was amazed to see how healthy the cattle were – I have never, before or since, seen adult cattle skipping around their paddock as these cows did. They didn't have just the usual ryegrass to eat, but a large variety of luxuriant herbs and grasses – red clover, plantain, chicory, all glowing with vitality. This vitality is an important indicator of health.

The animal you eat as meat was once alive and the quality of its life is reflected in the quality of the meat. A stress-free life in natural surroundings and minimal stress before slaughter results in better quality meat.

Taste and satisfaction

Often the large, unblemished fruit and vegetables in the shops have less taste than smaller, less 'perfect' ones. Or the taste may be different. I recently asked a group of school children to compare the taste of two sets of carrots – one bought in the supermarket, the other I grew organically in my garden. It appeared that the children who were used to eating home-grown vegetables preferred the flavour of the home-grown carrots: those who were used to eating bought vegetables said that the bought carrots were sweeter, without the stronger 'earthy' taste of the others. Many of us have become accustomed to the taste of simple sugars in vegetables and the strong, artificial flavours in processed food. The more subtle, complex tastes of garden fruit and vegetables that our grandparents were used to are less well known. So although our own taste should be the best indicator of quality, we may not be able to trust it if we have grown up eating processed or poorly grown food.

People who eat organic food often say it leaves them feeling more satisfied. That is also a good test – how quickly do you feel hungry again after eating a particular food? This satisfaction would at least partly relate to the dry matter content or quantity of nutrients in the food. New Zealand kiwifruit growers are paid more for kiwifruit with higher dry matter content because this has been found to relate to better taste of the fruit.

Taste and aroma

Your taste and smell are unique features of your individual make-up. Have you noticed how certain smells remind you of places or people? Geneticists have shown how we are attracted to someone of the opposite sex by smell, and that smell relates to their immune system (Strous & Shoenfeld 2006). We are attracted to someone with different immune system genes/potentialities so that children can inherit as wide a mix of immune system genes as possible, for better survival.

The aroma of food plays a big part in our food selection, enjoyment and digestion. The aroma from freshly baked bread or meat on a barbecue can easily make our mouths water.

As soon as food is smelt and tasted the digestive organs start secreting digestive enzymes. If a food has little aroma or taste it is more likely to cause indigestion because enzyme secretion has not been stimulated. Smell is linked to memory – the aroma of a particular food is associated with the memory of whether we enjoyed it or not. When we eat some food we not only taste it in our mouth, but our digestive organs 'taste' it as it passes through the digestive tract (Steiner 1991, p.13) and this is an important part of the digestive process.

Grazing animals have very acute smell and taste: these senses are vital for selecting food that is nutritious and not poisonous. Humans have less acute taste but are still able to recognise foods by their taste. We can train ourselves to be more conscious of our taste and to recognise how nutritious a food may be: generally the more alive with strong energies a food is, the stronger the taste.

Some people find strong tasting vegetables less enjoyable because they have become used to milder tastes of food grown quickly with soluble fertilisers. I have heard the view expressed that plants that have been bred to contain more water taste better, so people eat more of them. Those vegetables sometimes taste sweet, but it is generally the bland taste of simple sugars. Do you prefer to eat more, blander vegetables containing less nutrients or less, stronger tasting vegetables that have absorbed more light influence and developed higher quality nutrients? This is a serious question, because we are in danger of losing our traditional varieties of vegetables as large seed companies replace them with hybrid varieties that grow well in industrial farming conditions.

Vegetables grown less quickly and more naturally than many of the vegetables found in the supermarket, are often grown from heirloom seed and have developed higher complex sugar and protein content. They have a different, more complex, 'fuller-bodied' sweetness. A study of what determines carrot nutritional quality by scientists at Louis Bolk Institute in Holland (Northcote *et al.* 2004) put emphasis on taste. A sensory panel found that sweetness, carrot taste and juiciness decreased and acidity/astringency, bitterness and soapiness increased in carrots that were grown with large quantities of nitrogen fertiliser.

Artificial flavourings

Unfortunately the food processing industry produces a large range of chemicals that mimic the taste substances, fooling us into eating food that may not be good for us. When scientists analyse the chemicals in a taste and then copy it and put in artificial taste to food they are cheating our bodies. Not only are we cheated, but the chemicals are often harmful. There are an incredible number of flavourings and flavour enhancers added to processed foods. Many of the flavourings are copies of the main chemicals in natural flavours and do not have to be declared. They are generally added in much greater amounts than are found naturally so are more likely to be harmful. Eating food highly flavoured with artificial flavours confuses your own natural taste abilities so that you are less able to detect and be influenced by natural tastes in food.

Ripeness

The slogan 'good things take time' applies well to food. Compare the full flavours of an older chicken or well matured cheese with the tastelessness of a six-week old table chicken and cheaper, younger cheese. Researchers have also found what most of us have experienced, that harvesting fruit before it is ripe results in less aroma. Natural tastes are developed as a plant or animal matures, developing good protein, fats and oils.

We have a prolific old grapefruit tree in our garden. The fruit starts to ripen in June, but if there is not too much strong wind some fruit stay on the tree until December. By that time they are almost the colour of an orange and almost as sweet, with an incredible taste experience. Many children do not have such good taste experiences when eating fruit and vegetables that have been grown quickly, picked too soon, travelled some distance, set on a shop shelf and stored in a fridge for several days. No wonder many of them reject fruit and vegetables and prefer to eat manufactured hamburgers and biscuits.

Lessons from wine tasters

It is worth taking the trouble to train your senses to recognise high quality food. We can learn a lot from wine tasters who start by visual assessment and smelling the fragrance. The colour and texture are important. A good wine taster may take several minutes smelling a wine before tasting it. You can distinguish between healthy and rotting or other bad odours. The food should also have the right aroma for that particular food.

When tasting, wine tasters note the initial flavour, and then the flavour that lasts in the mouth. They record the taste sensation, such as dryness or warmth. A good piece of fruit or a vegetable should have complex flavours that give you a real taste experience, in the same way that good wines do. Tastes include sweet, sour, bitter, salty, dry, oily, astringent, pungent. The Slow Food Movement now provides education to help people develop taste experience.

It is the more complex components of food, developed as the product matures, that give it the taste. That is why food grown quickly with soluble fertilisers or fruit picked before it is ripe generally have little taste. Taste and smell relate strongly to the proteins in our food. If a vegetable does not have much taste it may have a very low protein content. The amino acids in protein have different tastes – many of them taste sweet but others taste bitter. Particular combinations of amino acids give characteristic tastes of a fruit or vegetable. For example, glutamate and aspartic acid give tomatoes their characteristic taste (Yamaguchi & Ninomiya 2000). A glutamate-to-aspartic acid ratio of 4:1 makes the tomato taste the best and brings out the genuine tomato taste. However, a well grown tomato would have more in its taste than just two chemical substances. Chemical analysis has shown at least a hundred chemical components of some tastes and fragrances. It is not the chemicals that are important but the living process that is producing the taste and fragrance.

The aroma you smell is from volatile oils which are a part of a living plant. The distinct fragrance and taste from a particular plant are aspects of the energies that a plant receives from the planets. For example, Steiner said the taste of apples comes from Jupiter energies (Steiner 1993, p.40).

The colour of a food is also a reflection of the energies in it. Colours such as the deep red of beetroot and purple of blueberries have been found to act as antioxidants in the human body. This antioxidant activity can be thought of as an energy activity. However, the energy effect from eating a particular food could be more specific to the eater than the general effects from colours. According to Gabriel Cousens (p.158) we are attracted to colours we need, to balance our own energies. He recommended eating different coloured food at different times of the day for a fully balanced diet.

A further aspect of wine tasting is to appreciate their *terroir.* This term applies to their uniqueness, reflecting the soil and environment of the particular place where they are grown. The soil type, for example whether it is clay or sand, affects the taste, but terroir relates to a particular vineyard. I think this term could be applied to food as well as wine. Some farms and orchards have developed their own food brands. Farmers' market stalls run by good farmers attract regular clientele who appreciate the taste and quality of their products.

In summary, when buying food, some important questions are:

—is it fresh or does it look old and wilted?

—how alive does the food appear – does it have a lustre?

—does it taste and smell good?

—for fruit, how ripe is it?

—where and how has it been grown?

—if it is in a packet, what additives does it contain and
  how has it been processed?

13. Growing High Quality Food

Home vegetable production

The best way to obtain really fresh food is to grow it yourself in your own garden. It's amazing how much can be grown in a small space. Most gardens have room for several vegetable beds and several fruit trees. Trees and vines can be tied along a fence or wall (espalier), and vegetables can be grown among flowers to look decorative. If you have good, well drained, soil you can dig it, add good quality compost to it, and you are ready to plant. Many home gardeners with less suitable soil make raised beds on top of their soil, using compost, straw, seaweed, grass cuttings, and so on. You can find instructions on how to do this on many websites such as 'No-Dig Gardening' (Carter, 2012).

Of course, the vegetables you grow will only be high quality if you grow them well, in soil with a good balance of nutrients. Regular spraying with organic sprays such as seaweed extract and weed teas helps to build strong plants. Weed teas are made by piling your weeds into a large metal drum, covering them with water and inserting biodynamic compost preparations into the mix. Sometimes it takes a few years to build up good soil and learn how to keep plants growing well, but most people find that once they start gardening it becomes easier and easier and very enjoyable and satisfying.

Many people now keep worm farms, which turn their kitchen scraps into a valuable fertiliser for the garden. If you have larger quantities of waste material in your garden you can build a compost heap.

Building a compost heap

Many people say they don't know how to build a compost heap, but it is actually very easy. You just have to follow a few basic principles. As well as providing nutrients for growing plants, a home compost heap enables you to recycle most of your kitchen waste, which otherwise contributes to pollution around landfills. Leave out meat scraps or you will attract rats, and don't include a lot of citrus skins which are harmful to compost organisms.

The secret of good composting is to build up thin layers of different materials. Intersperse fine materials such as grass mowings, weeds and kitchen waste with coarser materials such as twigs or straw. These trap air in the heap that enables the organisms that make the compost to breathe. They also need water, so keep the heap moist. Sprinkle a little good garden lime on your kitchen scraps to discourage flies and to feed the composting organisms. To increase the nutrient value of your compost add some animal manure or blood and bonemeal. I have found that most vegetables grow better if the compost contains animal manure. If you have access to seaweed from the beach that will add valuable trace elements.

To speed up decomposition, turn the heap every few weeks. Otherwise it will break down in six months to one year. More information about composting can be obtained from websites such as Garden Organic (Henry Doubleday Research Association n.d.) and ATTRA (2011).

The compost decomposition process can be enhanced by inserting the biodynamic compost preparations into the heap. These preparations provide energies that reduce the loss of nutrients such as nitrogen during the breakdown process. When the compost is incorporated in soil used to grow plants, it helps the plants to connect to the energies of the sun, planets and stars. Spraying the preparations 500 and 501 on soil and plants also enhance and balance growing energies, improving the nutritional quality of the plants. Details of how to make and use these preparations can be obtained in books such as Procter & Cole (1997) or from a

Biodynamic Association. The preparation 501 has an important effect on enhancing the 'light content' of food, which is discussed in Chapter 9.

Community and school gardens

Home and allotment gardening is increasing in popularity, but many people feel they don't have time to look after a garden. Some communities have solved this by setting up community gardens where everyone works for a few hours a week. In spring, 2008 a small group set out to create a community garden on a vacant piece of land in the small town of Thames, on the Coromandel peninsular, New Zealand. As the soil was possibly still contaminated with chemicals from goldmining days, raised beds lined with polythene had to be built. There is plenty of clay in the area, so the beds were surrounded by adobe walls built by enthusiastic volunteers at a workshop. The beds were filled with a mixture of cattle manure, seaweed, good topsoil and straw. After a few months a range of vegetable plants were planted.

Every Thursday morning there is a work session, at which the numbers of volunteers have steadily increased. A lot of vegetables are produced from this small area, for volunteers to take home, and to provide lunches on special occasions for the community.

Many schools are now making school gardens. Their children not only see and learn first-hand about looking after growing plants, they taste the results of their activities and are inspired to make gardens at home. In 2009 a committee of children at the Millar Avenue primary school, Paeroa, New Zealand decided to build school gardens as part of the Enviro-schools programme. They wanted to produce vegetables to share around the school and to grow flowers to make pleasant surroundings.

As the area available had little topsoil and there is plenty of clay in the area, they decided to build raised beds surrounded by adobe walls. An adobe wall expert gave a workshop and a large number of the children joined in building the walls, decorating them with sculptures and shells. The beds were filled with locally made compost, seaweed, rotted cow manure and topsoil. As many children as possible are given the opportunity to sow seeds and plant plants in the garden making a rather eclectic design, but a garden they have ownership of. When produce is ready it is harvested and used to supplement school lunches. Beetroot, cabbage and carrot coleslaw sandwiches are a great favourite. The children delight in experiencing new vegetables and watching worms and caterpillars around the garden. Strawberries are popular. Several of the children have asked for plots of their own in their home gardens and enjoy growing their own vegetables.

Another way to share the tasks of gardening and smallholding is through some kind of club or group activity. I belong to a group called 'Natural Growers' that has been running successfully in the Thames area of New Zealand for many years. Once a month on a Sunday morning, everyone in the group visits the property of one of the members, bringing tools, children, dogs and a contribution to lunch. We work on whatever tasks are requested for two hours, followed by a shared lunch. I find this a really enjoyable highlight of the month. It is an opportunity for socialising and catching up with friends in the group, but at the same time a lot is achieved. Whether it is clearing up and burning a tree that has fallen down, weeding the vegetable garden or helping to build new gardens, the group activity provides lots of enthusiasm and also pooled expertise: it is a good way to learn new ideas. Such a group could be set up by any group of town gardeners or small farmers.

There are groups in many areas that run workshops to teach gardening skills. The Soil Association in Britain and the Soil and Health Association in New Zealand advertise many of these. They are a great opportunity to meet like-minded people and learn new skills.

Every child should have the opportunity to eat fresh fruit and vegetables regularly and learn how they grow. That seems to me one of the most important things we can give our children as a basis for a healthy life.

14. Water Quality

We are waking up to the realisation that water is essential for life, that in many places it is in limited supply and that water pollution is a major problem. The quality of water that we and our animals drink, that we irrigate our crops with has a major bearing on our health. The quality of water used to irrigate crop plants is also important. Our bodies are around 60 % water and most of our food has a high water content. When we think about the food we eat and how it is grown in a wholistic way, all aspects of the water and air around us, the earth and sea of our world, can be seen to be inter-related, affecting our health and well-being. We want to buy food grown in a non-polluted environment.

When thinking about the quality of your drinking and plant irrigation water the first consideration is the source of water. Pure spring water is generally the highest quality. The water has matured through trickling down through the soil then moving up again until it reaches the soil surface. Many springs do not produce such mature water where trees have been removed from their catchment areas, exposing the land to heating and surface water run-off. Bore-water also has not risen through the soil so is less mature. Rainwater is even less mature as it has not passed through soil at all, and it is often polluted. Other sources of water are generally polluted or have been chemically treated. Many large cities are no longer able to source fresh water at all, it is recycled. Authorities take care to treat chemical and microbiological contamination but do not generally consider its vitality. Few people realise that water needs to have living, moving vitality in order to stimulate life in plants, animals and humans.

Characteristics of water

To think about water in a living, wholistic way we look at how it behaves naturally, rather than detailed analysis. The Austrian forester Viktor Schauberger studied water for many years. He pointed out that water flows naturally in curves, meanders and eddies, not in straight lines. It bubbles, swirls and chatters along, it looks alive. Every time water is forced into a straight pipe or canal it loses vitality. Schauberger emphasised the importance of the temperature and temperature gradient of water (Callum Coates, 1996, pp. 115–17). He studied the temperature of good spring water when it emerges from the ground, and found that it is around 4 degrees C, the temperature at which water is most dense, with highest energy content. When it flows under trees or in a deep river it maintains this temperature. If the trees are cleared and the water starts to warm up, it loses energy and coherence and provides the right environment for disease organisms.

The movement of water was studied extensively by Theodor Schwenk, who observed that water moves in constantly changing spiralling, vortex forms (Andreas Wilkens *et al.* p.25). Further characteristics of water described by Jochen Schwuchow *et al.* (pp.11–19) include its rhythmical flow and the ability to form clusters of molecules, which align into hydration layers in a coherent, crystalline structure. This structure holds energy and information.

Contact with pollutants destroys much of these characteristics of water. They can have a continuing contaminating effect which is difficult to remove. For example pollutants such as heavy metals and electromagnetic radiation change the information carried by the water so that even after those pollutants have been removed, the water retains a memory of them (Wilkens *et al.* p.14).

Assessing water quality

Andreas Schulz has demonstrated the effects of pollution on the structure of water, in his method of water crystallisation, freezing it into crystals. The structure and pattern of these water crystals provide a picture of the water vitality. Through the structures formed in these crystal pictures he has demonstrated how pollutants such as electricity and cell phone transmissions can reduce the quality of town water supplies (Schulz, p.15).

A further aspect that we do not usually consider in regard to water pollution is our thoughts. Masaru Emoto demonstrated how angry, hateful thoughts may be transmitted in water and change its structure when crystallised (Emoto 2004). Imagine the effects on the drinking water supply in a city where there is a lot of violence and unhappiness.

This capacity of water to hold the memory of thoughts can also be used beneficially. Water crystallisation picture show clear improvements in structure after water is blessed (Schulz p.154).

Another way to test water quality is through the water drop method developed by Theodor Schwenk, described by Wilkens *et al.* (pp.45–62). This method demonstrates how the water quality affects the way the water moves. A shallow layer of a water sample is mixed with glycerine and put in a shallow dish. A needle delivers regular standard drops of distilled water to the water surface. These drops set the water in motion, producing vertical patterns which are photographed regularly. The pictures show temporary ripple patterns which are regular and multi-formed in high quality water, but misshapen or unformed in polluted water (see Figure 14.1.).

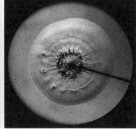

Figure 14.1: Water drop pictures of water from: left: mountain spring water, showing multiformed-rhythmical development; centre: mountain stream water, showing multi-formed to simple–leafed development, and right: waste-water-laden mountain stream showing ring to disc-shaped development. From Understanding Water *by Wilkens et al. (2002), Floris Books, p.70.*

Restoring vitality to water

There are many additives, gadgets and machines on the market that are claimed to restore water quality. It is beyond the scope of this book to discuss these here. One way that is increasingly used by farmers and gardeners is by restoring rhythm to the water. Water that is polluted or is passed through straight pipes loses its rhythm. When the biodynamic preparations 500 and 501 are stirred into water before applying to the land, they are stirred for one hour in a rhythmic way in order to restore rhythm and life.

An artistic way to restore rhythm to water was developed by the sculptor John Wilkes. He designed flowforms through which water is circulated (see Figure 14.2.). The shape of the flowforms is carefully designed so that water circulates round each one in a figure of eight pattern, developing a pulsating rhythm. Various flowform designs are obtainable for using for mixing liquid fertilisers, drinking water, food processing and for creating a restful ambience. These are described and illustrated in the book *Energising Water* by Jochen Schwuchow, John Wilkes and Iain Trousdell (pp. 48-52).

Figure 14.2: Flowform at Emerson College. From Flowforms, The Rhythmic Power of Water *by John Wilkes (2003), Floris Books, p. 115.*

When mixing a liquid fertiliser in our home garden using a flowform, some of the water splashed out around a lemon tree. This tree had hardly grown for several years after planting, in spite of trying various organic fertilisers. Shortly afterwards it started to grow vigorously, presumably responding to the flowform rhythm. Statistically designed trials carried out to compare plant growth when irrigated with flowform treated water or with non-treated water have shown that the flowform water increased root growth and sometimes the weight of the whole plant (Schwuchow *et al.* pp.71–94). Increased plant vitality and a stronger taste were observed.

15. Cooking to Maintain and Enhance Nutritional Value

In the preceding chapters we discussed the importance of the life energies in plants for nutrition. When you eat a salad of leaves fresh from the garden the energies from the living plant stimulate your own energies and keep you healthy. What about when vegetables are cooked? What happens to their energies? Tests using the picture-making methods described at the end of Chapter 7 have shown that good cooking, not too hot, is like a ripening process, making the vegetables more digestible and retaining life energies.

Cooking fuel and cooking container material

The effect of cooking varies according to what cooking fuel and containers are used. Rudolf Hauschka (2002, pp.150–54) related how he compared their effects on formative energy forces. He boiled distilled water in a reflux condenser using different kinds of fuel, or different materials of pot. The water was cooled and used to grow wheat seeds. After ten days the root and leaf growth were measured. He found that gold containers retained most energies, followed by earthenware, porcelain, enamel, glass, copper, tin, iron and aluminium. There was not much energy left after boiling in aluminium pots. He found that wood fires are best, gas is less good and electricity robs the vegetables of most of their energies. This research was done before the modern scientific methods were devised, but the results are interesting to think about.

Further research into cooking methods was carried out by

Christian Marcel. He used sensitive crystallisation to illustrate the organisational energies in foods cooked in different ways (Marcel 2009, pp. 89–95). His crystalline pictures showed interesting results in comparing green vegetables cooked by boiling, steaming and in a microwave oven. Those cooked in the microwave showed their organisational structure was less damaged than those boiled or steamed. Marcel concluded that for foods with high water content, the water molecules in the food are less agitated by microwaves than by boiling or steaming. However, when comparing frying with microwaving for apples, bananas, meat and salmon, he found that the microwave changed the organisational structure much more than did frying.

I notice a large difference in the taste and whole eating experience of root vegetables cooked slowly in an earthenware pot over a wood fire – a much more enjoyable experience, compared to electric oven cooking. Slow, low temperature cooking usually produces better tasting food. Hauschka also found that optimum cooking time varies with different types of vegetable. Vegetables that are flowers, like broccoli and cauliflower, need only a short time, after that they quickly lose formative energies.

Attitude and thoughts when preparing food

Thinking of fruit and vegetables as alive gives me a respect for them and the life they bring. Some religious teachings such as Hinduism incorporate this attitude of respect and thankfulness for the plants that give us food. Monks say prayers as they cook. Wendy Cook described how she learned the importance of how you cut and chop vegetables from Japanese cooks (2003, p.273). Chopping should be done in a quiet, ordered, rhythmical, conscious way, in a way that relates to the shape of the vegetable. The smaller the pieces, the more the flavour is lost in cooking water.

Like everything else in life, the attitude and mood you bring to cooking affects the result. Did you see the film *Like Water*

For Chocolate in which a young woman suffered terrible digestion because her sister who cooked the meals was very unhappy? The temperament and mood of the cook makes a great difference to the digestion and enjoyment of meals (Geuter 1962, pp.12–13). An impatient choleric cook tends to over-season the meal whereas a phlegmatic cook tends to produce too much, rather tasteless food. A meal cooked carefully with love is a great gift to your family who eat it.

These days we are busy with so many activities and most women work outside the home. It is hard to find the time for food preparation. But I think it is a question of making priorities. When you face the facts that most 'convenience' foods are highly processed, containing little or no life energies and that it makes a big difference to your family's health and thinking to cook high quality ingredients with love and care, then it seems worthwhile to find a way. Many people use slow cookers that can be prepared before going to work. Another possibility is to share cooking with friends or neighbours. I have found it saves a lot of time if I cook for a larger group less frequently instead of cooking for my own family every day, or if I provide only one dish to a shared meal. This has the added benefit of enjoying a relaxing social time while you eat.

Taking time to make the food look attractive also helps enjoyment and digestion. We are learning to do this, with so many TV chefs demonstrating recipes and presentation. The best chefs also take a lot of trouble to source really high quality ingredients. Harvesting fruit and vegetables fresh from your own garden, just before cooking, ensures that you are using high energy ingredients in your meals. A good alternative is to find a source of fresh fruit and vegetables such as a farmers' market.

16. Conclusions and Looking Forward

There is a growing sense of urgency worldwide to tackle nutrition issues. In 2008, twenty-six percent of the world's children under five were classified as moderate and severe underweight (UNICEF 2011). On the other hand, forty three million children under five (almost seven percent of the world's children) were estimated to be overweight or obese (Onis *et al.*, 2010). Their parents either lack the resources to obtain good food or they lack understanding of what is good food. It is now quite obvious there are serious problems from the alarming rise in obesity, and many other diseases. Nutrition is also a determining factor in cancers, allergies, mental health problems, criminal behaviour, drink and drug abuse.

It is time to recognise that:

The nutritional value of food varies considerably with how it is grown

Food plants grown quickly with large quantities of soluble
fertilisers contain more water and less nutrients,
organisational and light energies than plants grown
more slowly in biologically active soil.

Food is much more than a collection of nutrients: it is living energy

Eating all the right minerals and vitamins is not the
solution. Food supplements can have therapeutical uses
but are not a nutritional replacement for good food.
We need to think wholistically in terms of mineral and
energy processes dynamically interacting with each
other to produce living food. The unseen life processes

of earth, air, fire and water weaving through healthy,
living soil and around plants, produce healthy plants
that are sensitive to formative energies from the stars and
planets. Such plants contain vibrant, rhythmic, coherent
energy to provide nutritious food.

*We need more understanding of the life processes before we can
safely manipulate them*
An understanding of mineral processes and organisational
energies and how to work with nature to grow good
food is needed instead of attempting to mimic or replace
such processes in laboratories, factories and farms.

*We need more understanding of how silica assists plants to
incorporate light energies to build nutritious food*
When light is incorporated as coherent energy, food with
high inner quality is produced, containing high quality
protein and oils.

*We can learn to recognise good quality food by its taste, smell,
and appearance and we can learn to grow it ourselves*

High quality food is worth paying for
High quality food may take longer to grow and may cost
more than food grown more quickly with a lot of soluble
fertilisers but it contains more nutrients and living
energy so is worth more.

*The quality of food we eat affects not only our physical health,
but also our thinking, consciousness, emotional and
spiritual health and the health of our grandchildren*

We have a lot more to learn about life and living processes in our
world. We need to question, think for ourselves and investigate what
is the truth. Our scientific method has been developed to do this,

but it will only give the right answers if we ask the right questions, with a sense of wonder, reverence and awe at the beauty and intricacy of the plant and animal organisms that we often take for granted. We need to develop ways of enhancing nature rather than trying to fight or replace her. We need to apply the knowledge built up in quantum physics, that matter is made of energy, to biological sciences and nutrition. I have focused particularly on light energy, but there are many different energies, discussed in Chapter 5, that all need to be working and integrated to produce plant and animal foods with harmonious energies.

I find I have come on an amazing journey in writing this book, starting from questioning the statements that there is not much nutritional difference between eating organic and conventionally grown food, and that our food is short of light. Searching for the answer to one question opens up many more questions. The picture of food quality I have drawn together in this book draws together findings from many different disciplines: including traditional knowledge, conventional science, quantum physics, religious beliefs.

We may not be able to change the world, but each of us can choose how we eat. Are we going to consume more and more vitamin and mineral supplements or are we going to demand better quality food?

We, as food consumers, need to question whether our food has been grown with clean, living water and healthy soil. Was it grown by someone who cares for the health of their farm and animals and about producing good quality food for the people who eat it? Was the plant grown with care in healthy soil, rather than being force-fed in some artificial situation? Was the plant seed produced by natural breeding and selection or by genetic manipulation? Similarly, for animal food, did the animal live in the right conditions for that animal and eat high quality food itself? Did the farmer use tools such as the biodynamic preparations to help connect plants with the soil and with the stars and planets to provide strong, coherent energy? How can we support farmers who aim to grow high quality food?

162

Plants and animals grown with care to incorporate light and formative energies contain high quality protein, fats, oils and sugars. Food that is vibrating with strong light energies stimulates our inner light. This inner light maintains healthy organs and immune systems and enables clear thinking and consciousness.

It is the energy in food, rather than the chemical component, that is important for our nutrition. The energy that connects us to the earth we live on; to the light and warmth of spirit in the universe that surrounds us. When our food is grown in the right way its energy is harmonious and rhythmical, helping us to organise the energies of our bodies, to think clearly and fulfil our potential as human beings. Such food will enable us to be more emotionally, psychologically and spiritually healthy. It will help to reduce problems such as obesity and drug abuse.

I hope the time will soon come when the need for more harmonious, coherent energy in our food is well known and understood and the value of properly grown food is recognised. We all have a personal interest in ensuring that we eat the best quality food we can find, if not for ourselves, for the sake of our children, grandchildren and great-grandchildren.

Bibliography

Adams, George H. & Whicher, O. (1980) *The Plant between Sun and Earth,* Rudolf Steiner Press, London.

Allport, Susan (2006) 'The Queen of Fats: Why Omega-3s were removed from the Western Diet and what we can do to replace them' *California Studies in Food and Culture,* 15, pp.115-50.

Anderson, Jennifer & Roach, J. (2010) 'Food vs. Pills,' *Colorado State University Extension Factsheet* no. 9.338.

Atkinson, Glen (1989) *Astrological Science,* http://old.garudabd.org/books/ Accessed 7.1.12.

ATTRA (National Sustainable Agriculture Information Service), USA, (2011) *Soils & Compost,* http://attra.ncat.org/soils.html/ Accessed 13.1.12.

Aukema, Harold & Aluko, R. (2009) Effects of a novel pea protein hydrolysate on hypertension and chronic kidney disease, at the *American Chemical Society's 237th National Meeting* Utah, USA. http://www.pulsecanada.com/uploads/a8/93/a893e71b45553363e6a0b6f1255c7a0a/09-Aluko-Aukema-pea-protein-hypertension-ACS.pdf/ Accessed 10.1.12.

Balzer-Graf, Ursula (1999) *Quality and communication for the organic market,* Sixth IFOAM Organic Trade Conference, Florence, Italy.

Barnes, M.J. (1975) Function of ascorbic acid in collagen metabolism *Annals of the New York Academy of Sciences* Volume 258, Second Conference on Vitamin C pp. 264–77.

Bischof, Marco (1995) *Biophotons – The Light in Our Cells,* Zweitauserdeins, Frankfurt. Published in German. English short description, http://www.marcobischof.com/en/arbeitsgebiete/biophotonen.htmlhttp://www.marcobiscmar.com/en/arbeitsgebiete/biophotonen.html Accessed 14.1.12.

Bloksma, Joke, Northolt, M., Huber, M., Jansonius, P., Zanen, M. (2004) *Parameters for apple quality-2 and development of the inner quality concept.* Louis Bolk Instituut, Publ.no. GV V04.

Bohm, David (1980) *Wholeness and the Implicate Order,* Routledge, London.

Brennan, Barbara A. (1987) *Hands of Light,* Bantam Books, New York.

Carter, Megan (2012) *No dig gardening*, http://www.no-dig-vegetablegarden.com/raised-vegetable-garden.html Accessed 13.1.12.

Cheraskin, Emanuel *et al.* (1994) Establishing a suggested optimum nutrition allowance (SONA); What is optimum? *Optimum Nutrition Magazine* 7 (2) 46–47.

Coates, Callum (1996) *Living Energies*, Gateway Books, Bath, UK.

Coghland, Andy (1994) 'Good vibrations give plants excitations', *New Scientist Magazine* Vol. 192 Issue 1927.

Cole, Gillian L.(2003) *Investigation of relationships through which biodynamic growing practices affect plant growth and nutrient composition.* Thesis for M.Sc. Massey University, New Zealand.

Cook, Wendy E. (2003) *Foodwise,* Clairview Books, East Sussex, UK.

Cousens, Gabriel (2000) *Conscious Eating,* North Atlantic Books, California.

Culpeper, Nicholas (1995) *Culpeper's Complete Herbal*, Wordsworth Editions Ltd., England. (original edition 1653).

Ellis, Kathryn A. Innocent, G., Grove-White, D., Cripps, P., McLean, W.G., Howard, C.V., Mihm, M. (2006) Comparing the Fatty Acid Composition of Organic and Conventional Milk. *Journal of Dairy Science* 89:1938–1950.

Emoto, Masaru (2004) *The Hidden Messages in Water,* Beyond Words Publishing Inc., Oregon, USA.

Endres, Klaus-Peter & Schad, W. (2002) *Moon Rhythms in Nature*, Floris Books, Edinburgh.

Engel, Greg S., Clahoun, T.R., Read, E.L., Ahn, T., Mancal, T., Cheng, Y., Blakenship, R.E., Fleming, G.R. (2007) Evidence for wavelike energy transfer through quantum coherence in photosynthetic systems, *Nature,* 446, pp.782–86.

Fallon, Sally & Enig, M.G. (2000A) *Nourishing Traditions*, Ashtree Publications, Woodstock, New York, pp.253ff.

—, (2000B) 'Newest research on why you should avoid soy', *Nexus Magazine,* Vol. 7, No. 3 (April-May 2000).

FAO/WHO (1985) *Energy and protein requirements*. Report of a Joint FAO/WHO/UNU Expert Consultation, World Health Organization Technical Report Series 724 Geneva. Section 7.3.3.

Gerber, Richard (2001) *Vibrational Medicine*, Bear & Company, New York.

Geuter, Marie (1962) *Herbs in Nutrition*, Bio-Dynamic Agricultural Association, London.

Goethe, Johann W. (1978) (originally published in 1790) *The Metamorphosis of Plants*, Leo F. Manfred Associates, Inc., USA.

Harrill, Rex (1994) *Using a refractometer to test the quality of fruits and vegetables*. Pineknoll Publishing, Keedysville, USA. http://crossroads. ws/brixbook/BBook.htm/ Accessed 5.1.12.

Hauschka, Rudolf (1998) *Nutrition: a holistic approach,* Sophia Books, East Sussex. UK.

—, (2002) *The Nature of Substance: Spirit and Matter*, Rudolf Steiner Press, London.

Heaton, Shane (2002) 'Assessing organic food quality: is it better for you?' In Powell *et al.* (eds.) *UK Organic Research 2002: Proceedings of the COR Conference, 2002*, Aberystwth, pp 55-60.

Henry Doubleday Research Association, (n.d.), Garden Organic, How to make compost, http://www.gardenorganic.org.uk/organicgardening/ compost_pf.php/ Accessed 13.1.12.

Holford, Patrick (2004) *The New Optimum Nutrition Bible*, Crossing Press, Berkeley, Toronto.

Howard, Judy (1990) *The Bach Flower Remedies Step by Step,* C.W. Daniel Company Ltd., Saffron Waldon, Essex, England.

Huber, Karin (2004) Klosterstudie – *Food Quality Research : How does food quality affect body, soul and spirit?* Forschungsring für Biologisch-Dynamische Wirtschaftsweise, Darmstad, Germany. http://www.biodynamic.org.uk/ certification/research/food-qualities.html accessed 5.1.12.

Ingham, Elaine R., Moldenke, A.R., Edwards, C.A. (2000) *The Soil Biology Primer*, Soil and Water Conservation Society, USDA NRCS, USA.

IARC (International Agency for Research on Cancer) WHO (2004) *Cruciferous vegetables, isothiocyanates and indoles*, IARC Press.

Juge, Nathalie, Narbad, A., Lucchini, S., (n.d.) *Integrated biology of the GI tract* http://www.ifr.ac.uk/info/science/git/gut-microbiota.htm Accessed 9.1.12.

Kaufmann, Klaus (1993) *Silica, The Forgotten Nutrient*, Alive Books, Canada.

Klotsche, Charles (1992) *Color Medicine*, Light Technology Publishing, Flagstaff, AZ, USA.

Kolisko, Eugen (1978) *Nutrition No.1*, Kolisko Archive Publications, Bournemouth, England.

—, & Kolisko L. (1978) *Agriculture of Tomorrow*. Second edition (originally published 1939, Gloucester, John Jennings). Kolisko Archive Publications, Bournemouth, England.

Kranich, Ernst M. (1984) *Planetary Influences upon Plants*, Biodynamic Farming and Gardening Association Inc. Kimberton, USA.

Koenig, Uli J. (1988) *Investigation of phenomena of diurnal rhythms and developmental dynamics with selected crops after application of biodynamic spray preparations*, PhD-Thesis, University of Goettingen, Germany.

Koepf, Herbert H. (1993) *Research in Biodynamic Agriculture: methods and results*, Biodynamic Farming and Gardening Association Inc., Kimberton, USA.

Laane, Henk-Maarten (2008) Silicon for humans: beneficial or essential? Silicon in Agriculture Conference 2008, South Africa, p.59.

Lauterwasser, Alexander (2006) *Water Sound Images*, First English Edition, Macromedia Publishing, Newmarket, USA.

Liberman, Jacob (1991) *Light Medicine of the Future*, Bear & Company, Rochester, Vermont, USA, p.59.

Lillo, Cathrine, Appenroth, K.J. (2001) Light regulation of nitrate reductase in higher plants: which photoreceptors are involved, *Plant Biology* 3(5), pp.455–65.

Lipton, Bruce (2005) *The Biology of Belief*, Mountain of Love/Elite Books, Santa Rosa, USA.

Lloyd, David, Aon, M.A., Cortassa, S. (2001) Why Homeodynamics, not Homeostasis? *The Scientific World*, 1, pp.133–45.

Louis Bolk Institute (2011) *The Koala Project: is organic food healthier?* http://www.louisbolk.org/research-2/healthcare-and-nutrition/nutrition/Koala-research/ Accessed 6.1.12.

Marcel, Christian (2011) *Sensitive Crystallisation*, Floris Books, Edinburgh, UK.

Marieb, Elaine N. (1998) *Human Anatomy and Physiology*. Fourth Edition, Addison Wesley Longman, Inc. California.

Marti, Ernst (1984) *The Four Ethers*, Schaumburg Publications, USA.

Mercola, Joseph & Droege, R. (2004) *The Real Reasons Why Raw Milk is Becoming More Popular* http://www.mercola.com/2004/apr/24/raw_milk.htm/ Accessed 5.1.12.

Meyer, Anne-Marie (1997) Historical changes in the mineral content of fruits and vegetables: a cause for concern? In: *Agricultural Production and Nutrition*. Proceedings of an international conference, Boston, Mass.

Mitchell, Alyson E., Hong, Y., Koh, E., Barrett, D.M., Bryant, D.E., Denison, R.F., Kaffka, S. (2007) Ten-Year Comparison of the Influence of Organic and Conventional Crop Management Practices on the Content of Flavonoids in Tomatoes *J. Agric. Food Chem.*, 55 (15).

Northcote, Martin, van der Burgt, G., Bulsman, T., Bogaerde, A.V. (2004) *Parameters for Carrot Quality,* Louis Bolk Institute, Drieburgen, The Netherlands.

Onis, Mercedes de, Blössner, M., Borghi, E. (2010) Global prevalence and trends of overweight and obesity among preschool children, *American Journal of Clinical Nutrition* 92:1257–64.

Pelikan, Wilhelm (1997) *Healing Plants*, Mercury Press, Spring Valley, New York, p.25.

Pembrey, Marcus E. (2002) Time to take epigenetic inheritance seriously, *European Journal of Human Genetics,*10, pp.669–71.

Pettersson, Bo D. (1978) A comparison between conventional and biodynamic farming systems as indicated by yields and quality. *Proceedings of the International Research Conference* IFOAM, Wirz Verlag, Aarau.

Pfeiffer, Ehrenfried (1936) *Formative Forces in Crystallisation*, Rudolf Steiner Publishing Co., London.

—, (1958) *Sub-nature and super-nature in the physiology of plant and man*, Mercury Press, Spring Valley, New York.

—, (1984) *Chromatography applied to quality testing*, Bio-dynamic Farming and Gardening Association, Inc., USA.

Price, Weston A. (1939) *Nutrition and Physical Degeneration*, Price-Pottenger Nutrition Foundation, USA, pp.275-76.

Pollen, Michael (2009) *Food Rules: An Eater's Manual*, Penguin Press. New York.

Popp, Fritz-Albert (1994) Biophoton emission: experimental background and theoretical approaches, *Modern Physics Letters B*, Vol. 8, pp. 1269–96.

—, (1998) 'The physical background and the informational character of biophoton emission.' In *Biophotons* (eds.) Chiang, J.J. *et al.* Kluwer Academic Publishers, Netherlands, pp.239–49.

Pottenger, Francis M. (1983) *Pottenger's Cats: A Study in Nutrition*, Price-Pottenger Nutrition Foundation Inc., USA. pp.9–44.

Procter, Peter & Cole G.L. (1997) *Grasp the Nettle,* Random House, New Zealand.

Reffitt, David, M., Ogston, N., Jugdaohsingh, R., Cheung, H.F.J, Evans, B.A.J, Thompson, R.P.H, Powell, J.J., Hampson, G.N. (2003) 'Orthosilicic acid stimulates collagen type 1 synthesis and osteoblastic differentiation in human osteoblast-like cells in vitro,' *Bone*, Vol. 32, Iss 2, pp.127–35.

Remer, Nikolai (1995) *Laws of Life in Agriculture,* trans. Castellitz K., Davies B. Bio-Dynamic Farming and Gardening Association Incs. Kimberton, USA.

Ren, Huifeng, Endo, H., Hayashi, T., (2001) Antioxidative and antimutagenic activities and polyphenol content of pesticide-free and organically cultivated green vegetables using water-soluble chitosan as a soil modifier and leaf surface spray. *Journal of the Science of Food and Agriculture*, 81, 15, 1426-1432.

Schlosser, Eric & Pollan, M. (2008) *Food, Inc.* DVD http://www.foodincmovie.com

Schmidt, Dorian (2005) *Observations in the field of formative forces in nature,* Biodynamic Agricultural Association, Stroud, UK.

Schulz, Andreas (2003) *Water Crystals*, Floris Books, Edinburgh, UK.

Schweitzer, Albert (1961) *Civilisation and Ethics*, Unwin Books, London, pp. 212–31.

Schwenk, Theodor (1965) *Sensitive Chaos*, Rudolf Steiner Press, London.

Schwuchow, Jochen, Wilkes, J., Trousdell, I. (2010) *Energizing Water*, Sophia Books, Forest Row, UK.

Shaw, Peter (1988) 'Wheat quality – Putting the N into protein,' *Riverina Outlook Conference*, Southern NSW, Australia.

Shayne, Vic (2000) *Whole Food Nutrition: The Missing Link in Vitamin Therapy,* iUniverse.com Inc, Lincoln, USA

Sheldrake, Rupert (2009) *A New Science of Life*, third edition Icon Books, Omnibus Business Centre, London.

Simopoulos, Artemis P. (2002) The importance of the ratio of omega 6/ omega 3 essential fatty acids *Biomedicine & Pharmacotherapy* 56 (8) pp.365–79.

Somers, G. Fred, Beeson, K.C. (1948) The influence of climate and fertilizer practices upon the vitamin and mineral content of vegetables. *Advances in Food Research*, 1, pp.29–324.

Steiner, Rudolf (1921) *Anthroposophical spiritual science and medical therapy,* Lecture 9, Steiner archives. http://wn.rsarchive.org/Lectures/ GA313/English/MP1991/19210418p02.html Accessed 18.1.12.

—, (1972) *An Outline of Occult Science*, Anthroposophic Press, New York.

—, (1980) The supersensible being of man and the evolution of mankind, *Anthroposophical Review*, Vol. 2, No. 3, GA 330.

—, (1982) The Spiritual-Scientific Basis of Goethe's work, GA35 http:// wn.rsarchive.org/Articles/SSBoGW_index.html Accessed 18.1.12.

—, (1989) *Spiritual Science and Medicine*, Steinerbooks, Blauvelt, New York, USA.

—, (1991) *Nutrition and Stimulants,* Bio-dynamic Farming and Gardening Association Inc., Kimberton USA.

—, (1993) *Agriculture.* A series of lectures given in 1924. Gardner, M. (ed.).Translated by Creager, C.E., Gardner, M., Bio-Dynamic Farming and Gardening Association Inc., Kimberton, USA.

Strous, Rael D. & Shoenfeld, Y. (2006) 'To smell the immune system: Olfaction, autoimmunity and brain involvement,' *Autoimmunity Reviews,* Volume 6, Issue 1. pp.54–60.

Stolz, Peter, Stube, J., Buchmann, M., Hiss, C. (2000) Better dietary protein-quality of beans cultivated biodynamically than by hydro-culture. In: Alföldi, T., Lockeretz, W., Niggli, U. (eds.). IFOAM 2000: *the World grows organic.* Proceedings of the 13th International IFOAM Scientific Conference vdf Hochschulverlag AG an der ETH Zurich.

Thijs, C., A. Müller, L. Rist, I. Kummeling, B.E.P. Snijders, M.A.S. Huber, R. van Ree, A.P. Simões-Wüst, P.C. Dagnelie, P.A. van den Brandt (2010) Fatty acids in breast milk and development of atopic eczema and allergic sensitisation in infancy, *Allergy*, 66(1), pp.58–67.

Thun, Maria (2003) *Results from the biodynamic sowing and planting calendar,* English Edition, Floris Books, Edinburgh.

Triglia, Antonio, La Malfa, G., Musumeci, F., Leonardi, C., Scordino, A. (1998) 'Delayed Luminescence as an Indicator of Tomato Fruit Quality,' *Journal of Food Science*, Vol. 63, No. 3, pp.512–15.

UNICEF (2012) *The State of the World's Children 201, Statistical Tables 2011: Table 2 Nutrition,* UNICEF, New York

United Nations, Department for Economic and Social Affairs, Population Division (2005) World Population Prospects: The 2004 Revision, New York, pp.2–3.

USDA (2011) USDA National Nutrient Database for Standard Reference, Release 24 http://www.ars.usda.gov/main/site_main. htm?modecode=12-35-45-00/ Accessed 5.1.12

Walsh, Lance P., McCormick, C., Martin, C., Stocco, D.M. (2000) Roundup Inhibits Steroidogenesis by Disrupting Steroidogenic Acute Regulatory Protein Expression – StAR *Environment Health Perspectives* 108.

Watanabe, S., Fujiwara, T., Yoneyama, T., Hayashi, H. (2001) Effects of silicon nutrition on metabolism and translocation of nutrients in rice plants. In: Horst, W.J. *et al.* (eds) *Plant nutrition-Food security and sustainability of agro-ecosystems,* Kluwer Academic Publishers, Netherlands, pp.174–75.

Watson, George (1972) *Nutrition and your Mind,* HarperCollins, New York.

Wilkens, Andreas, Jacobi, M., Schwenk, W. (2002) *Understanding Water,* Floris Books, Edinburgh, UK.

Wolcott, William L. & Fahey, T. (2000) *The Metabolic Typing Diet,* Broadway Books, New York.

Wolf, Reik W. & Walter, J. (2001) 'Genomic imprinting: parental influence on the genome,' *Nature Reviews: Genetics* Vol.2, pp.21–32.

Yamaguchi, Shizuko & Ninomiya, K. (2000) 'Umami and Food Palatability,' *Journal of Nutrition,* 130:921S–926S.

Index